LETTERS FROM PRISON

selected and translated by Gerald Turner

LETTERS FROM PRISON

MILAN ŠIMEČKA

TWISTED SPOON PRESS
PRAGUE • 2002

ISBN 80-86264-03-3

PREFACE

We first met Milan Šimečka in May of 1990 when he flew to New York with our friend Jiří Hanzelka, the famous Czech writer and dissident. They had worked and suffered together with Václav Havel and the few other active dissidents who helped to bring down the Czechoslovak Communist regime in November 1989. They had come to Bard College in the Hudson Valley for one of the first conferences in America on the 1989 revolutions in Eastern Europe.

It was Hanzelka's and Šimečka's first visit to America, so we invited them after the conference to our home in nearby New Paltz, on their way to New York City and their return home.

We vividly remember Šimečka's insistence that he had to see New York City "before I die." So, we got a driver and Czech speaker to show him the great sights of New York before he flew home to Bratislava, where he died four months later of a heart attack.

After the Russian invasion of 1968 squashed the Prague Spring campaign to reform Czechoslovak Communism, Hanzelka was not allowed to publish any of his worldwide travel books; Šimečka could not publish his philosophical writings about utopias, political freedom, and telling the truth except in limited circulation internal samizdat or publication of his books and essays in Europe or America.

Milan Šimečka looked you in the eye with his penetrating gaze, spoke the truth and demanded it in return. We were deeply impressed by his honesty and moral courage, and the fact that he was one of the best writers of the Czechoslovak dissident movement.

We read parts of his book *The Restoration of Order*, his analysis of the Soviet crackdown on the Prague Spring. But we did not discover the power and beauty of his personal writing until we read translations in English of two letters he wrote to his family from Prague's Ruzyně Prison in 1982, after he was sentenced to ten years in jail by the Communist authorities for activity against the State.

Those two letters from prison were translated for us by Dagmar Kusá, daughter of Miroslav Kusý, another Slovak dissident, while we were sponsoring her for a year's study at Bard College in 1997-98. Her translation was based on the original edition, in Czech and Slovak, of many more letters, published in 1999 by the Milan Šimečka Foundation in Bratislava.

Dagmar told us stories of playing ping-pong as a little girl with Milan Šimečka at the Kusý home in Bratislava during meetings in the 1980s of many Czech and Slovak dissidents. These meetings were watched and often broken up by the police. Dagmar knew Šimečka in moments of warm personal charm and later appreciated the literary quality of his letters from prison and their universal human interest. It was she who provided the inspiration for this English translation of Milan Šimečka's *Letters from Prison*.

We thank Dagmar Kusá, Gerald Turner and Howard Sidenberg at Twisted Spoon Press for helping us bring these fascinating letters to English-speaking readers.

—Jim and Mary Ottaway
New Paltz, New York, September 2001

Jim and Mary Ottaway have visited Prague since the 1989 revolution, and have sponsored students from the Czech and Slovak Republics for study at Bard College every year since 1991. Mary is a teacher and artist. Jim is an American newspaper publisher, senior vice president of Dow Jones and Company, chairman of its Ottaway Newspaper group, and chairman of the World Press Freedom Committee.

FOREWORD*

I knew Milan Šimečka at the beginning of the seventies, that is, at the beginning of the period of "normalization." It was Milan who wrote what is perhaps the most thorough analysis of the entire normalization era. His book, *The Restoration of Order*, is an excellent analysis of the situation that prevailed at that time. It has a certain phenomenological touch but is, at the same time, very readable.

Throughout the entire 1970s and 80s Milan Šimečka and I took part in the meetings of writers who were then banned and who later began to publish the journal *Obsah*. He regularly came to these meetings from Slovakia. The meetings took place nearly every month, certainly several times a year, in various locations, always in someone's country house or apartment, and in a practice that quickly became a tradition, he presented his political analysis of the situation at the start of each meeting. Many of us derided him for being perennially over-optimistic, but his presentations were always frank, thoughtful, perhaps a little too impassioned, and always admirable for their remarkable scope.

Šimečka was a sensitive and perceptive man who took everything to heart — indeed, his sensitivity to others made one feel a sense of well-being in his presence. Nevertheless, this did not mean that his analyses ever succumbed to excessive emotion, nor did he get upset or overly excited by our debates. He managed to rise above whatever subject was then under dispute in a calm, deliberate, and matter-of-fact manner — as if he were watching all this worldly commotion from someplace higher up. He was above things.

After some time had passed, Milan Šimečka and I met again for a brief period, when I invited him to work at Prague Castle as an adviser. It was those first, revolutionary days, when the Presidential Chancellory was

* Originally written for *Nová Přítomnost* and *Kritika & Kontext*, no. 3-4 (1999), pp. 86-87; translated by Samuel Abrahám and reprinted here with his and the author's kind permission.

still not a proper office, when everything was improvised, and when we were still searching for the right way to do things. For half a year he headed the team of my advisers. He died suddenly, unexpectedly; we were all shocked. I remember how we all flew to Bratislava to attend his funeral.

I confess that today I miss his frank views of political events. It would have been good if he could have stayed with us a few years longer.

—*Václav Havel*
President of the Czech Republic

CONTENTS

INTRODUCTION

During the period of the Czechoslovak Socialist Republic, prison letters had a strictly prescribed format. In the top right-hand corner was the name and address of the recipient, in the top left-hand corner the name of the sender, i.e., a detainee or convicted prisoner, his/her date of birth, and the address of the prison. Letters to prison had to observe the same format, except that the left and right corners were reversed.

In the case of my own correspondence with Milan Šimečka when we were both held in the same prison — at Ruzyně, near Prague Airport — the layout was particularly ludicrous. The address of the sender and the recipient were exactly the same: Prison No.1, Ruzyně, P.O.B. 614/09 — 16102. We were both held in the same block, and our cells could have easily been just ten yards or so apart. But we definitely weren't on the same floor. Women were on the first floor, men were on the floors above.

Every fourteen days we were allowed to write just one letter and always to the same address. I wrote to my children; Milan Šimečka wrote to his wife, Eva, and via her to his friends and relations. Václav Havel, who was held at Heřmanice, Bory, etc., used to send his letters to his wife, Olga.

I knew Milan Šimečka before his imprisonment. I used to arrange for manuscripts of his books and essays by him and other Slovak writers to be sent to the West, chiefly to his long-standing friend Vilém Prečan, who was then in exile and responsible for editing and publishing a number of texts. We didn't admit to that at interrogations, of course. But I wanted to know how Milan was making out! We couldn't use the "traditional" prison method of passing a note through the bars (the note is put in a sock and the recipient tries to pull it up to the higher floor), and there was no way of sending a message by knocking on the plumbing — he was never on the floor immediately above me! So I made a special request for permission to send a letter also to him from time to time. It was granted.

That first letter about "defense mechanisms, or how to survive prison" was returned straight to me by my interrogator even though it was couched in very general terms. I knew that letters like that were carefully "studied" by our handlers, so I then wrote to Milan about Hegel and consoled him and myself with examples of how knowledge and conscience liberate humans from slavery, drawing him a couple of pictures to show him that I wasn't too badly off. That second letter was passed on to him. And I even received a reply to it. However, my interrogator only permitted me to read it. After confirming in writing that I had seen and read it I then had to hand it back. In my letter I had drawn Milan a flower, a poppy doll and "Mole" from the children's cartoon, and he told me in his reply that he didn't know I could draw. Letters of that kind were permitted by the censors. The important thing was that we knew about the other!

Readers of Milan Šimečka's prison letters might also be familiar with other writings of his and could be puzzled how someone so kind and decent came to be behind bars! Why was he forced to share a cell with murderers, arsonists, and robbers? The reason was simple. A group of ten of us were arrested for writing and sending texts abroad and charged with breaching Paragraph 98 of the Criminal Code (Subversion of the Republic). Absurd? No, at that time it was "normal"!! After all, it was the period of "normalization" — the official term used by the leaders of the then Communist establishment for their neo-Stalinist policies. The Prague Spring of 1968 — i.e., the attempt to reform socialism and give it a "human face" — was branded as treason. So the return to socialism on the Soviet model with no freedom of the press or even any opportunity to discuss different ideas, and everything again under the absolute control of the Communist Party, was described as "normal" or alternatively as "real socialism."

Today, over ten years since the fall of the Communist regime, even I, who spent most of my life in totalitarian regimes without freedom, find it impossible to understand how it was possible to imprison people for sending their book manuscripts abroad, for translating George Orwell or Hannah Arendt, for writing political essays about Andrei Sakharov, Solzhenitsyn, or Heinrich Böll, lending the magazines *Svědectví* published in Paris or *Listy* published in Rome, or reading Milan Kundera's novels published in Czech in exile, or A. J. Liehm's article about the "three generations." It was sufficient for three people to testify before the court that a text incited them against the socialist order and the author could be convicted. When the secret police (the StB) found in someone's apartment a book or magazine published abroad by a Czech exile publishing house, it was confiscated and the person was interrogated about where they had obtained the publication. Even during the normalization period after the occupation of Czechoslovakia in 1968 one could not be prosecuted for merely reading a text! But to divulge who gave it to you could cause that person serious difficulties. So we would say we had found the manuscript or magazine in our mailbox or on the doormat, or even on a park bench, but above all we'd stress that we had not given it to anyone else to read.

The regime was powerful but also powerless. When, for instance, a group of friends who were assumed to be opponents of the regime regularly met in someone's apartment or a pub, the secret police would detain them as they were leaving, check their identity and take down their details. Sometimes they would be taken off to the police station and have their bags, handbags, pockets, notebooks, diaries searched, particularly for lists of friends. This fostered an atmosphere of fear in which people retreated into their private lives and humiliated themselves in various ways. At the same time, it could stiffen the resistance of others and spur them into reflecting on this reality and finding some way of sending the results of their reflections abroad. Where they were successful, our friends in exile saw to the translation and publication of texts and books and endeavored to place articles by banned writers in the Western press. The aim was to "prove" to the West that the population of Czechoslovakia was not entirely apathetic and acquiescent. The more such articles were published, the more people wrote! Every writer needs feedback; there is no pleasure in writing solely "for the desk drawer" and some eventual readership. Creative people need others to react to their texts!

The links with the exile community were forged slowly and in stages. However, within a few years the new exiles managed to set up a number of publishing houses and organize the translation and publication of smuggled manuscripts. This in turn encouraged other authors back home to resume their writing and led to the creation of an "independent" literature (which subsequently found a temporary home in the Documentation Centre for the Promotion of Independent Czechoslovak Literature, set up at Scheinfeld, Bavaria, by the exiled historian Vilém Prečan.) But first it was necessary for all these texts — analyses, manuscripts, and the archives of those who had emigrated — to be gotten out of the country and into the hands of the Czechoslovak exiles. By then a considerable number of foreign tourists and "pseudo-tourists" were visiting Czechoslovakia. The latter sort would travel from London, Vienna, Paris, Rome, Amsterdam, Hanover to collect manuscripts and deliver books and magazines published by the Czechoslovak exiles. The Cold War was still in progress, but Stalin was nearly thirty years dead. The country was still ringed by barbed wire and electric fences, but the representatives of the regime wanted to trade with the West. Broadcasts by Radio Free Europe, BBC, Voice of America, and Deutsche Welle suffered jamming, but something got through! The isolation was not complete.

Palach Press was set up in London around 1972, and from then on several times a year — and later every five weeks — a specially adapted van with concealed compartments would travel from London to Prague carrying about 200 kilograms of books and other literature. It would return to England with manuscripts and articles that would then be published in the West and return here in printed form to be secretly distributed. And the seemingly all-powerful secret police were foxed. They knew that thousands of copies of "anti-socialist" literature were circulating among people but didn't know how it got here. They were unable to find "the channel." It wasn't until the autumn of 1980 that a prisoner who had been convicted of political offences (specifically,

Ruthenian nationalism) submitted to pressure from the secret police and agreed to cooperate with them. When he was released from Mírov Prison — one of the toughest in those days — he started to mix with the dissidents. Eventually he was able to inform the police that a vanload of books was due to cross the frontier at the end of April 1981. And so it came about that a van driven by two members of the French Human Rights League was stopped at the border and then stripped and dismantled. It was the first time the van had failed to reach Prague! It stood to reason that news of it would eventually leak out. By May 8 State Security had arrested and detained on remand some fifty people from the Czech and Slovak republics. They included Milan Šimečka's close friend, the Slovak philosopher Miroslav Kusý, the former Foreign Minister Jiří Hájek, the future post-Communist Minister of the Interior, Jan Ruml, as well as former student leaders like Jiří Muller, not to mention journalists such as Karel Kyncl, who in later exile achieved enormous popularity among the Czech and Slovak public as a BBC broadcaster. The detainees also included Václav Havel's wife, Olga, and his brother, Ivan, who were organizers of a samizdat publishing operation. (Václav Havel himself was already in prison at the time, having received a four-year sentence in October 1979 for Subversion of the Republic.) I, too, was arrested as the coordinator of the "channel" and a sort of "postman" between the exiles and the people here. For our activity we were all charged under Paragraph 98 of the Criminal Code (Subversion of the Republic as an organized group), for which the minimum penalty was three years imprisonment and the maximum ten.

Our arrest came at a time of international "détente" and when Solidarity had achieved recognition in Poland. Our friends in the Czechoslovak exile community widely publicized our plight and leading western politicians, including such heads of state as Thatcher, Mitterrand, Kreisky, Brandt, and Reagan were fully informed, as a result of which the Czechoslovak regime was told that future trade and diplomatic relations with those countries were at risk unless we were released. The secret police had scored a success, but they had bitten off more than they could chew. They certainly had in their hands evidence of the existence of resistance to the regime in the form of a large group of intellectuals. However it was also evidence for the Soviet leadership under Leonid Brezhnev that normalization in Czechoslovakia was not a total success. So the Soviet Union itself was not altogether pleased. As a result, most of those arrested were released on remand after several weeks, leaving only eight of us in Ruzyně Prison. The report of the secret police interrogations ran to thousands of pages and the evidence of our "guilt" filled forty-two files. Eventually the rest of us were released without trial a year later. The indictment was not cancelled officially until Václav Havel became president, when we received an official notification that the charges had been dropped and we were not allowed to appeal the decision. We obeyed the president!

President Havel then went on to invite the former political prisoner, Milan Šimečka, to join his team of advisers with special responsibility for Czech-Slovak relations. Just a few months later, Šimečka was "summoned" on the basis of an unknown, but eternally applicable law, against which there is no appeal, and he died of a heart attack on September 24, 1990.

For me and for many of our mutual friends, Milan Šimečka remains a kind, gentle, and understanding "personal superego" to whom we often turn with the importunate question: "Well, what do you say about how things are going, Milan?"

Šimečka's *Letters from Prison* give us some idea of how he might have responded to the present state of affairs. In them he was not allowed to mention politics, so he wrote about people, love, and human relations. The selection of letters presented here bears witness to his attitude to other people, to his imprisonment and the period in which he lived, as well as his personal philosophy. Maybe precisely because the letters were written from prison they are not "overburdened with everyday problems and pseudo-problems," but are written with detachment and reflect on questions that we all ask ourselves from time to time.

—Jiřina Šiklová

LETTERS FROM PRISON

courtesy of Jolana Kusá

Picnic by the Rudava River, Slovakia, 1983. From the left: Milan (Martin) Šimečka, his wife Marta, Petr Šimečka, Eva Šimečková, Dagmar Kusá, Jolana Kusá, Milan Šimečka.

9.13.81

When they dressed me in the stinking shirt I'd slept in for four nights and the trousers that are now too big for me, I started to suspect I would see you. I waited, locked in some office, and I shivered all over. I can't ever remember waiting for something with such agitation in all my life. And then when I set eyes on you it was like being run over by a train. Your living presence cancelled out my prison existence. Everything was suddenly rewound back . . . But anyway, you know the state I was in, you could read it in my face. What a terrible shame Milan[1] wasn't with you and instead was standing up to his waist in mud. I expect I'd have been ashamed if he'd seen the tears pouring down my cheeks. (But so what — the last time I cried was when Fredo[2] died.) I can't remember what we talked about. I can recall only fragments. I don't even know what I said, but it certainly wasn't what I wanted most to say. But what should one say, anyway? Let's forget it. I expect you saw for yourselves how dear you are to me, and I could tell, too. That's the main thing, and the rest isn't so important. After you left I yearned to be alone for three hours to let it all sink in, but I had to wait until the evening siren went and I pretended to be asleep in order to play back every minute of the visit, every glance, every handclasp, every hug. Half an hour! I think we all discovered that time can be used as an instrument of torture. Petr[3] looked fine, but you, Eva, my love, looked gaunt and your eyes gleamed in your tanned face.

It was only when I received your letters that I discovered how shocked you were by my appearance. I realized it two days after your departure, because I was summoned to the doctor. They weighed me and asked if

1. Milan: Milan Šimečka, Jr. (b. 1957).
2. Fredo: Šimečka's brother Alfred (1922-72).
3. Petr: Šimečka's elder son (b. 1956).

I had an appetite and so on, something that is so out of the ordinary that I guessed you must have written to someone, dissatisfied that I was at last slim enough to be one hundred percent attractive to you. I told the doctor and I'm telling you too: *I'm all right!* And I ask you with utter sincerity not to grieve over fifteen kilos of surplus flesh and fat. I'm happy to have gotten rid of it all without any strenuous jogging to Železná studnička. I doubt if anyone leaves prison rejuvenated and looking better. I eat normally. Not like at home, of course, but I don't go hungry and I'm not even choosy. I simply lost weight pining for you, nature, decency, and many other things. But I'm not ill. Lizzie[4] lost weight too, the time she got lost. I explained it all to the doctor and we agreed he was unable to prescribe the medicine I needed. So forget about it, Muki,[5] and stop fretting over the loss of a few proteins, fats, and water, because, as we know, it's the soul that counts. I'm joking a bit, but you really shouldn't be worried.

Your visit was followed by a lavish feast. They allowed me to take back to my cell everything you brought, and on top of that your parcel had arrived. So I was well stocked up. It was a real feast day! Those divine turnovers! I still manage to squeeze out a bit of honey for my morning slice of bread. I must have put on at least a couple of kilos! Shortly afterwards I got Petr's letter, then the French textbook, and then, with unexpected promptness, the letters you wrote after the visit. So the last two weeks have been very eventful, which is good in prison terms.

This time you wrote me a lot, especially Petr. I've already written to you on many occasions about the private ceremony I make out of reading your letters and how I subject them to profound textual analysis. I remember them almost word for word and they are my greatest comfort. The same goes for your photos.

My love, all I can do is to go on begging you to realize that your grief and anxiety only do you harm and don't do me any good. I know it's easy to say. But you must try. I'm sure you've discussed it with the boys

4. Lizzie: the Šimečkas' cat.

5. Muki: Šimečka's pet name for his wife, Eva (b. 1931).

lots of times. Try to take their advice and adopt their philosophy. I've always held the view that people should always be governed by positive feelings. The sorrow and despair apparent in your letters are negative feelings, even though they are the other side of your love. But they are able to wreak as much damage to the soul as jealousy, envy, selfishness, or hate. I expect you read what Petr wrote me when he described sailing down the branch of the Danube. I take that philosophy at its full worth. Try to learn it. All I need to be happy is the knowledge that I have a caring, loving, and brave wife standing by me. I don't need a sorrowful and careworn wife as well. I'm sure you know what I mean. It's a long time since I've stopped thinking about a specific moment in the future when I'll come home. But if we're lucky enough to have such a moment, I'd like to find you as unchanged as possible. God knows what I'll look like! Try to indulge this little selfishness of mine. Otherwise I take all your advice and fully appreciate it. Thank you so much for doing all you can to help. Do you know how fantastic it is to submerge myself in something as abstract and divorced from prison life as French grammar? It's a spiritual bath. I also get pleasure from every photo and postcard. Kudrna's postcard from Dartmoor was a real achievement. Goodness knows what it looks like there. It would make an interesting comparison. And it immediately occurred to me that it must have been taken from the very spot where the two of us stood and looked. As if it might have struck me at the time that years afterwards some sort of thread would connect that place with my private destiny. What most shocked me on those photos was how young we were. What were we in those days? Ordinary tourists. If I'd had my present experience behind me at that time, how much more splendid it would have been! I even examine in detail postcards from Valašské Meziříčí and recall where I once used to park on the square there.

9.19.81

It's Sunday and I sit down to write this letter after a sleepless night. Maybe it was the coffee, though more likely the excitement of your visit. I spent the night talking to you and told you all sorts of things, everything I didn't manage to tell you during that half hour. If I were to write it all down it would take me a week non-stop. So I won't even try. By now I've got so many monologues that I'll never manage to write them all down. And who knows whether it would be worth it.

And now I was planning to say something to you, Milan, about your letter and the picture. I thought it would be ages before we saw each other again. And all of a sudden here you were with your new ginger beard. And once again I couldn't believe my eyes that it was you sitting there. I remember you telling me that you are leading a happy life. And that's precisely my wish. In fact I knew already, because I always suspected somehow that you'd manage to lead a life outside of the usual conventions, which means that adversity won't unsettle you. And my guess is that it's a life rich in love and the sort of human situations that adversity engenders. I'm glad you have lots of friends and are able to savor the things that cease to be available when you reach so-called responsible adulthood. And again I know that you don't need to be told it.

Naturally I was bowled over by the thought that I might become a grandfather in prison. Except that the happy-go-lucky prison existence makes you perceive things differently and you adopt no attitude to what's going on, because the way people live outside seems like a film and quite unrelated to you. So I was chiefly taken by the fact that my dream about a child coincided with the belated and inaccurate news. By now I'm even capable of thinking that your main preoccupation at the time somehow managed to penetrate these walls and create that unusual dream for me. The only reason I mention it is I don't think anything of the kind has ever happened to me before. The sense of tenderness and joy that I felt as I leaned over the child was so powerful that I awoke with my eyes full of tears. Where did it come from, I asked myself. At first I thought it might be the cosmic child from Arthur C. Clarke's *2001: A Space Odyssey*, but now I think it would be rather lovely if it were actually a dream coat that your overriding preoccupation dressed itself in, here in this cell. And it was a marvelous dream coat, or rather that old-fashioned bathrobe with the splendid gold stripes that I saw as a child and I think belonged to my mother. I think that Marta would be happy with my dream. I can imagine what they all said to you, but it's over and done with now.

It's good that you find selling knives and kitchenware interesting, although it's unlikely to be as good a source of literary inspiration as the hospital. You know how much I'd love to chat with you about literature. I think I've learned more about it here than in my entire life previously. Understood more than learned. Previously I perceived literature as a sort of wide stream of colourful lights that merged together. I would roam among them and have trouble distinguishing between them in terms of value or staying power. In prison the soul has a more intense perception of everything. I suddenly feel cosmic distances between the value of the books I read. I read Victor Hugo's *Les Misérables*, for instance, and suddenly realized that in spite of its fame it is no more than a sentimental story for philanthropic fanatics. Or I'm reading Balzac again, although I read all his works ages ago. And all of sudden I realize that *Lost Illusions* is awfully descriptive. True, one learns everything about finances in the publishing world, as well as lots of interesting things about the manufacture of paper, but you also discover that Lucien is no more than a figure, a dummy clothed in a literary lesson about standardization. And then you happen to come across a copy of *War and Peace*, something you think you know inside out — after all there have been so many film versions of it. And as you read it and get deeper into the book you sense what enormous literature it is. When Mother and I were translating Forster, and he kept repeating that there was this Russian count with his message and then for a long time nothing, I thought to myself: Wait a moment, wait a moment, I've read him. But it was only here that I realized what a giant he is and how alongside him all those literary discussions about methods and the nitpicking of modern criticism are so paltry. Because the chief miracle is that when Bezukhov is observing the Battle of Borodino, the madness of the human race epitomized in a single battle, it is I along with him who am filled with human despair and am incapable of grasping the sense of history; it is not just his amazement and horror, it is also mine. And then when Andrei dies with a crushed pelvis, you die with him, too. Natasha comes towards you. First she's like a white speck by the door in her nightgown, maybe with the face of Audrey Hepburn. But it's not Natasha, it's all the happiness you've ever known, all the love, everything of value, everything human. That scene encapsulates the whole of Tolstoy's philosophy of love. Everything can be understood without theorizing. And that's what literature really is. When I was reading that scene I had to turn my face to the wall lest my cell-mates see a prisoner letting himself stupidly get upset over some tattered old Russian book. Read the scene with Marta and let me know if it has the same effect in the lamplight on the couch with a glass of wine and the occasional kiss, or whether it's just the effect of this prison cell. In the end, scruples aside, anyone with a bit of perceptiveness was aware of that anyway. But how easily one forgets such things in this crazy world.

9.26.81

I now sit down to write with a touch less discouragement. They've told me I can write once a week, which has cheered me up a lot. There is now a lot more hope that you'll receive some of my letters after all. Apart from which, as you know, my defense counsel came to see me. On the Prosecutor's advice I am to send my letters to him and he will forward them to you. I'm accordingly sending a covering letter to the Prosecutor's office along those lines. So I can start off on a rather more hopeful note.

Mind you, autumn isn't really the most hopeful season of the year. Almost every morning Ruzyně is covered in mist and I can see the leaves turning yellow on the few trees here. I only know about last summer from the papers. I know you went bathing a lot and that it was terribly hot again in our attic apartment. Otherwise I don't know a thing about the summer. My cell is strangely unaffected by the weather. It is not just cut off from human society, it is cut off from nature, too. As if it were somehow out of this world.

Apart from a lot of other things I have come to understand here, I have fully come to realize the enormous importance of nature in human lives. I now understand the vital role it plays in the health of the human personality. For months now I have listened to talk in which various inward yearnings of all my different fellow-lodgers have surfaced. And for months I have waited for someone to say something to do with nature, to voice a longing for the peace of summer, sun, water or even a garden, but have heard nothing of the sort the entire time I've been here. There is not even a reference to nature in any of the different tales I've heard. As if nature were completely divorced from the lives of those people and played no role at all in them. As you might imagine, the most recurrent yearnings concern beer, food, women, tape recorders, discotheques, civilized adventures, etc. And suddenly it occurs to me whether this lack of any feeling for nature has a causal connection with their social and human disorders.

There you are, and as I ponder this my mind goes back to the sad visions of Rousseau and Thoreau, and even Marx's theory of alienation, and in fact all those warnings about how alienation from nature can play havoc with humans. And what I once took to be slightly exaggerated and nostalgic notions about the lost harmony of man and nature now sounds to me like a specific and tangible cause of the malignant disorders of our civilization. I also no longer consider those various friends of nature that we would meet on our travels as oddballs but as champions of humanity. I'm even beginning to think that even the average Joe who takes the cable car up to Lomnické sedlo[6] and is bowled over by the view of the valley is already on the way to victory in his battle with life. And maybe it's a hard and fast rule that you only meet good people on the ridgeway between Prašivá and Chabenec.[7] This definition is not altered by the fact

6. In the High Tatra mountains.
7. Locations in the Low Tatra mountains.

that you are liable to get your skis stolen. That's another matter.

I'm possibly saying things we all know, but the awful thing is that we regard them as part of our general knowledge of the world. Except that I hear tales of hopeless human situations, and there are more and more of them, and I'm already beginning to formulate a simple theory which might be backed up by sociological research and unshakeable statistics: Save nature and you'll save the human race. But this theory is not worth a thing unless . . . Nonetheless, family allowances should only be paid to parents who take their kids into the woods at least once a month to observe the strivings of ants with them.

But for heaven's sake, I wasn't intending to write to you about my theories. Originally I just wanted to tell you how therapeutic it is for me in the peace of the night to recall ecstatic moments associated with nature that still make me tingle as much as they did then. And thank God there were plenty of them. It is sheer delight to be back again in that half-ruined village high above the sea. Do you remember, Eva? We were visiting some Slovenian painter whose children were asleep on sheepskins on the stove. And after a few glasses of red wine we climbed up onto some ramparts and from there you could see the lights of fishing boats reflected on the surface of the sea, otherwise invisible in the darkness. And above them shone the Mediterranean stars. In addition I could feel beneath my feet that ancient turf, trodden perhaps by some Roman slave as he went for water. Everything — nature, my consciousness, and the whole of human civilization — fused into a single moment of rapture. But the main thing is that it all came back to visit me in my cell, and I wallowed in that memory like in a feather bed. And I couldn't even smell the latrine.

I already wrote to you that if at some future moment — which I don't think about for the time being — we'll be together and allowed to go wherever we like, you'll have no difficulty in dragging me away from my books and work into some ordinary woods with ordinary trees and footpaths I know by heart. On the contrary, I'll dash off as soon as I can to see a slug crossing a path, leaving behind itself a slimy trail. For a long time we kept a spider here, a leggy creature by the name of Joanna. I would watch it move around the ceiling. For hours and hours it would hang from one spot. One day it disappeared. It probably crept into some hole behind the light. I expect spiders enter a state of physical and mental torpor for the winter. If I could learn to do it too how blissful I would be. But I don't know if I'd really want to.

9.27.81

They've changed the time here, too. It was bright this morning but the evening will be that much darker, not that it makes any difference here anyway.

I've already thanked you many times for your letters and written various comments on them, which you never received. I was taken by many things in those letters. Such as ordinary tenderness, for instance. A pity that Petr never read my thanks for what he wrote me. He seemed a new person in those letters, more mature, philosophical, and emotionally open. I often read those letters over and over again and their atmosphere transports me back all those months. They are like the remaining pages of a calendar.

I discussed those letters with you and I still would be able to. When Milan confesses his dread of the laziness and torpor of summertime, I can see him before me with that eternal restlessness in his eyes, afraid he'll miss something. I'm lucky to have a different mental constitution. What would I do with that sort of restlessness here? There really is nothing to do here and time passes like some totally useless attribute of space. I already hate it as a philosophical category. It's like glue; it sticks to my fingers and my soul. I suddenly perceive it as a living creature with a slimy, indolent body that lounges around here, filling the narrow space until it's impossible to breathe. When I was small and got a fever I would always wake from my sleep in a state of terror because some swelling mass, dark and alive, like the belly of an antediluvian creature, was rolling on top of me. Only now do I realize that that creature was time. Only now have I come to know that monster intimately. It is actually an enormous leech that feeds on the time of our lives, both mine and no doubt yours too, my love. Because you know best of all that we have time in common. It's your leech, too.

But let's think about something more human. Milan's beloved looks at me out of the photo with large eyes. I have incorporated her with you into my former world. And I am happy inside that they experience their love so intensely. It would be lovely if I could run with you in the last of the summer wind and be as fast as he is, and share that feeling of being in a glass bell. What is wind?

Milan, you divulge some of the petty jealousies that assail you. This new civilized jealousy that only causes a slight scratching of the heart has its uses. It prevents one from becoming complacent in love. But full-scale jealousy is a real swine that roots around in human relations with its snout and makes a total quagmire of them. I have been through petty jealousies in my time and enjoyed them. However, your mother might tell an unhappier tale about them.

Nevertheless, son, it has been my view for a good few years now that jealousy is a challenge to one's intellect. It's a test that a strong intellect should cope with. What does a man lose by the fact that the woman he loves is attractive to others? Nothing. On the contrary, he gains. Go ahead and admire her. At the same time you're admiring me because this woman loves me. The rest of you merely make her life more pleasant. Naturally that only applies to relations between civilized individuals. I'd be ashamed to relate such esoteric matters in a cell where tales are told of sexual promiscuity so complicated that it is difficult to make head or tail of them. Sometimes I truly start to forget that there exists another world that has its own moral standards. More than one world, in fact. But I much prefer the one illuminated by reason. And in that one the jealous person is an object of pity. At the end of the day, jealousy always betrays a secret sense of inferiority. Not sexual, but intellectual. I'm not sure whether that fits in with the Freud you're now reading, but all my observations of life convince me of it. When I was being escorted here, my ill-informed guard tried to persuade me that my wife would inevitably be unfaithful to me, quite simply because that's what all women are like. And he told me a hundred stories from life to prove it. I just nodded, because even if we had been bound for the furthest corners of the earth, I would have never managed to convince him that there was another reality apart from the world of his stories. It is deciphered from primitive shorthand into an articulated pattern, and I won't allow anything from that sequence to be removed or overturned. Sometimes, son, I think it's preferable to die rather than abandon that pattern. Because once one has achieved a pattern of reality based on reason and education, the only way one can descend into another reality is through human degradation. But that is another philosophy. And all this on account of a reference to jealousy!

10.3.81
[A letter for his son Milan's birthday]

Well, now it's the turn of your birthday. Twenty-four years: a splendid and slightly paltry total for someone like me. But in your case this age doesn't seem to me insignificant. Ever since you were fifteen or thereabouts I've always thought of you as being more mature and prepared for your age. It's because ever since then the going has been rougher for you in life's race than for others. Apart from that I loaded you down with rather more intellectual baggage than was wise. But that was all due to circumstances. Somehow I automatically assumed you would cope and come to terms with it, and that you'd emerge stronger from those trials, that you'd make sense of it, that you were quite simply built for clearing hurdles and would actually get pleasure from it. And in fact it's only now, after I've come across different philosophies of life, that I realize you were as perfectly entitled as anyone else to say: I've had enough! Screw it, I couldn't give a shit about all your fine words, fuck all your highfalutin philosophy, all your literary truths and refinement that don't buy a thing. I've got a right to live like everybody else instead of always having to come to terms with things, having to be better and more sensible. Fuck it.

The words I use are the ones I'm surrounded by and are severe in their way. The greatest miracle of our life is that you never said them. I have to confess myself that I was so naive at the time that it never occurred to me that you might adopt such an attitude. Only now do I see that it is the most common attitude of your generation. That was mainly the reason why, when you were in your teens, I thought of you (cruelly maybe) as a twenty-year-old and soon afterwards as a grown man. So it's only in respect of others that those twenty-four years seem paltry to me. In reality you're much older than I was at the age of twenty-four, because although I was already married and a university graduate, I was essentially a naive young man. You are older by a different era and different conditions of life. But let's not say older, let's say riper: that word has a better ring to it and means more. Ripeness is something to be savored, since maturity is the basis for coping with life and enjoying it to the full. So I congratulate you on your ripeness, my child!

You already know from my conversations with Mother that you were rather special as a child. More self-reliant than Petr and independent. Whenever I looked into your eyes when you were five or ten years old I always had the feeling that something was going on behind them that was not appropriate for a child of that age. It struck me that those eyes held a foreboding of things that I couldn't understand and yet you would tackle them in your own way. We have a few photographs at home on which those eyes are noticeable. We were accustomed to them, but once we received a visit from a young woman who happened to have a baneful effect on our family life. You were at home playing with marbles. That young woman took a look at your eyes and said: "Just look at his eyes. He frightens me." And she left and never came back. You could have been four at the time. An odd story. Odd, too, that I've never forgotten it.

When I run through all the things I remember from your childhood, I am amazed to find that there are no painful memories. It's a happy story from start to finish. What I mean is that you yourself were never the cause of disappointment or misgivings. The only source of resentment was what afflicted you from outside: childhood illnesses and official disapproval.

You yourself only provided a few minor challenges to my pedagogical efforts, leaving me at a loss when I was unsuccessful. Such as when I tried to get you to swallow a mouthful of meat you'd chewed dry. I did everything I could, but I knew that in the end I'd let you spit it out into the garbage pail. You would gaze at me sadly but make it clear that there were things between heaven and earth that the human will was powerless to budge, and one of them was chewed meat. And that scene would be repeated quite often, though not with chewed meat, of course.

I recall how for some time you were obsessed with the idea that you were a foundling, that you didn't belong to us, that you weren't ours. And I have to admit that there were times when I'd watch you in disbelief and marvel at the laws of inheritance. Such as when you taught yourself to read and write without our particularly noticing it. Or when you came in from school, set your exercise books out on the table, and got on with your homework. And there was no budging you. It struck me as a sort of infantile obsession, a sense of duty that I'd never had. I put it all down to the maternal inheritance. Or when you were at vocational school, how you would go off to bed at nine o'clock in the middle of a TV thriller because you had a training session at six the next morning. Or when you were only ten and went to the dentist before school in the morning to have him put fillings into your crumbly teeth. And I asked you why you were getting up so early and you simply declared that you were going to the dentist's. At such moments I would feel quite an absurd sense of esteem for my own child. I don't know how many fathers have felt something similar.

I felt the same thing when I watched you learning to ski. Or when you swam in a calm sea right out to the shark barrier just a couple of days after you learned to stay afloat. And many other times too! Oddly enough, even then I realized that your engrossment in some particular activity was not for the benefit of possible onlookers, such as me or your mother. You weren't angling for praise, you did it all on your own account. It used to strike me that you were in constant dialogue with yourself and you simply needed to confirm something you learned about yourself from that dialogue. And you didn't get it from books, either. I don't think you were ever very much taken by Jack London's he-man stuff and I was always pleased to see you preferred to learn Tom Sawyer or Huckleberry Finn by heart.

The actual reason I'm saying all this is that now, more than ever before, I am aware of the relativity of child rearing. It was all inside you irrespective of us. I already wrote to Petr on his birthday what a boon it was for me that I sometimes allowed you to instruct me and discovered more than once how the world assumes more acceptable proportions in the light of childish artlessness. Parents who fail to realize that the education of their children is a two-way process generally come to grief. Our family has retained its rare cohesion because Mother and I were able, maybe not entirely consciously, to submit to your influence. I wrote about it in detail to Petr — a pity the letter was lost. I provided there a few fine examples of parental pomposity.

Maybe I ought to comment in this letter on something that was always the subject of my discussions with Mother and which we called *Schuldgefühle*.[8] I would suppress my feelings of guilt by dint of reason where possible. And you would assist me enormously. The trouble was that I couldn't avoid what Maxim Gorky described as "toothache in the heart." There were plenty of such occasions, but I can still remember the moment when I found you at the age of fifteen weeping on the couch because they hadn't accepted you for high school.[9]

We were already able to explain everything else in comfortable, rational terms. With varying degrees of success. You are absolutely clear about it in your mind just as I am and know what it amounts to. When you think about it, we spend our entire lives doing the strangest things, and each time we sustain a wound we use our reason as a salve; it helps a bit, but not altogether. I already have great experience with this procedure and have made good use of it. It has helped me to overcome minor panic attacks. It's good experience, and it can serve you throughout your

8. Schuldgefühle: a sense of guilt.
9. He was not accepted because of his father's political record.

life and even transport you rationally through the last, inescapable complication of this life into non-existence. But we both also know that even the most complex logically structured arguments are not all-powerful and old wounds do hurt a bit even years later. Naturally I have my old feelings of guilt here with me, sitting alongside me. And sometimes I'm quite pleased to be able to tell them: Look here, after all those family accidents I am now the worst cripple of all. At least I have some defense. But I say it with a touch of self-irony, so don't take it too seriously. If all those wounds now hurt less than they did, it's not because of me, but above all thanks to you (and maybe Marta, too).

Quite simply, the overall feeling on your twentieth-fourth birthday is one of peace. Joy and relief and many other delightful feelings. I feel as if I've been on a really long run to Železná studnička that has lasted several years and it's behind us now. My body is overcome with a delicious exhaustion, warmth, and torpor, and I can already hear my strength being renewed. I can hear it in my beating heart as it sends oxygen to my muscles. It's something you know best of all, and I have confirmed it here. I exercise till I drop and then have a wash. And my body simulates all the feelings of a long run. All I lack is the chance to stretch out on the couch in our room. We are fully aware, of course, that there'll be another run after this and then another, but by now we know what we're doing and look forward to the torpor and the trembling muscles.

I hope this isn't too confused for you to understand what I was getting at. After all your running you're so fit that you don't need advice from me. I feel as if all I should do now is sit among the spectators and keep my fingers crossed for you. Maybe the others don't yet know how much you have trained. I do, which is why I'm calm and can only look forward with relish to your future races. And maybe you'll let me run up to the fence and advise you in which lap you should put on a bit of a spurt.

I could name a whole lot of events on which I base my calm assurance, and my part in them, starting with your training at Slovnaft,[10] swimming,

10. Slovnaft: the Slovak state petroleum monopoly.

athletics, military service, and the hospital and ending with literature and Marta. It all seemed to me like a series of minor works. I was there at the beginning and watched them grow with pleasure.

But I didn't only enjoy the way you coped with that obstacle course. Since I have an almost pathological esteem for reason and human intelligence, what pleased me most of all were all the manifestations of those "good fairies" of yours. I knew about them from the outset, of course, but they never failed to amaze me. And of course I felt an undeserved genetic pride. I've already written to you about it in a letter. They probably didn't give it to you so that you wouldn't get a swollen head. Oh yes, it was the time I commented on the debate you had with Petr about the significance of knowledge of technology and arts. I don't feel like repeating it.

Naturally I'm aware of the advantages of a specialization which university can provide to a certain extent, but I intuitively give priority to universal knowledge that comes from curiosity and universal intelligence. I feel there is a shortage of such knowledge in the world, and the lack of it is partly the cause of mankind's present maladies. Maybe the fact that you couldn't acquire that specialized education opened for you the way to universal knowledge, which is not lucrative but can help you live a fuller and happier life. In any case, we'll see how it all turns out.

It wouldn't be me if I didn't leave the joys of literature to the end. When you first started to write us those long letters from military service I suddenly had the feeling that something had been decided. I realized that you were unable to resist the challenge of a provocatively white sheet of paper. What you wrote us was more than news. You were starting to give shape to your perception of the world and trying to grasp reality in such a way as to recreate it on paper. It wasn't simply an entertaining experiment in controlling words, but on the contrary a first attempt to cope with an unclear and hostile reality, undertaken in the realization that the written word is the only medium specially designed for it. Because the word is the logos, even if we no longer want to believe that in the beginning was the Word and it was God's property. You had the right approach, and at first I didn't comment on it — out of fear of transferring my guilt to you and your becoming its unwilling captive. And you know best of all that it came of its own accord. The fact that we subsequently worked on it a bit together is another matter; it was just a question of craftsmanship. It was all an adventure for me, too. Like following the development of a chrysalis. I tried to maintain a cool, neutral, and non-committal approach, knowing that in our circumstances all sorts of things lay in wait for the butterfly that would emerge from that chrysalis. But I didn't manage to be an entirely neutral spectator. You can't be neutral when it comes to literature. But you're aware that I tried not to exaggerate your first training sessions and declare you the winner in advance.

I have tested on many occasions the particular perceptiveness for text that I have developed over the years. I don't maintain that it is an ability to identify a great literary work on first sight. It's more complex. It's rather an ability to sense the enigmatic radiation of some text, even when it is only something short, a fragment, just a few sentences. Whenever I detect some note, a slight trembling of the soul, a touch of beauty, some little novelty, whatever it is that transforms lines of text into literature, I feel it like wind in my face, like the warmth in my stomach after a glass of wine, simply as something that defies definition but exists nonetheless.

And that happened to me that time when I was reading your letters. And many times since. In the first stories, the accounts of brief moments. It is odd how I remember it all. For instance that winter, and the cold, the frozen grass, the aircraft lights, and the stars above your head. Or the warmth of Helena's apartment. The feeling of the thick carpet between the toes of your bare feet, the coffee cup, and time measured in the passage of the sun across the apartment blocks opposite. See, I remember it all. It's here with me. What would I give now to be able to walk barefoot across a carpet! I know what it was like. I also know how to celebrate an ordinary experience that others are unable to perceive. Because first they have to have a cold impersonal floor beneath their feet.

I knew already back then and I silently rejoiced. Who would have understood it? After all, there was no money in it, it wasn't food or drink, it wasn't even a new coat or a new girlfriend. Simply balm for the soul. And yet I think back on it as one of the most splendid things I've experienced in recent years. A pity there was no one for me to share it with; or more accurately, I was shy to share it with anyone and instead made a show of indulgent forbearance.

I have always tended to go for the beauty of detail in literature. When all the fine detail is assembled it is easier to construct from them the whole. After all, what do we remember from literature? Only the details, which we never forget and which spring forth when needed. Stories get forgotten, but not the fine, sparkling details. The same goes for life. From a long journey, for instance, we can remember a single postcard, the smell of beans cooking on a stove, or a pool of pure water with dace basking in the sun.

I know it's not easy to create the whole out of fragments of reality. But I knew it would come in time. It was my hunch and also my wish. I also thought that the story from the hospital actually created its own structure through the power of its marvelous detail. A blue tent to make love in, the autumn air above the paths of Železná studnička, and the tiny open bosom of a young girl, which I cannot forget here. You know, son, I may have a few bad traits here and there, but I've never understood or experienced myself what is termed literary envy. I have always un-selfishly relished what others have achieved and would happily shower affection and praise on such a fortunate. So all the greater was my enjoyment of your story, and only pedagogical forbearance kept my feet on the ground.

Well, I've told you plenty. And it's all part of my peace of mind on the occasion of your twentieth-fourth birthday. Because, after all, by now everything that will happen is only an attendant circumstance of a fixed run. And whoever knows how to run and has kept in training will win a medal one day.

As I sit here thinking about you I fully believe what you said during your visit about being happy. It sounds like blasphemy after all we've been through, but I believe quite sincerely that you don't have to feel bad about your twentieth-fourth birthday. I am thinking of Marta, who is with you, and all the remarkable features of the life you lead. And I'm sure you already realize that in fact it's all one needs. When I think of all the unnecessary things people drag through life with them! How easily and happily I'd go off and be a hermit today if your mother would go with me and the two of you would visit us from time to time. And if I had a typewriter there and the papers and a drop of wine and a good radio and halušky with bryndza cheese.[11]

There's loads more I could write, old pal. When I remember everything it seems to me like reading some book. All I need to do is slowly copy it out. But I've committed myself to sticking within these thirty little pages. Think up some celebration so that I know the surroundings and can be there with you. I'll sit here quietly and drink a toast. And from time to time I'll slap you on the back and stroke Marta's hair. Cheerio, my boy!

11.14.81

It's ages since I received anything from you and none of the announced letters arrived, but what's the point of grumbling? I've already got used to the fact that my letters and yours are a kind of monologue whose fate is not determined by us. I've been wondering if I should write some Christmas cards but was appalled how time was flying, so I thought I'd leave it for next time perhaps. In the meantime, then, I'll just ask about things — as if I expected an answer. But there's no need for one; most of the answers I know already. But I feel like asking questions, because I'm slowly starting to doubt the existence of certain phenomena and paraphernalia of my life. Their long-term absence from my present existence makes me start to doubt my memory, which insists that things still exist as before. Just like the medieval mariner, who after months

---

11. Halušky: Slovak potato gnocchi; bryndza: soft sheep's cheese.

sailing the seas would cease to believe that dry land existed any longer, I'm gradually ceasing to believe that certain things exist. My memory provides no more than an abstract testimony, which increasingly lacks sensory evidence. If they amputate your nose, smelling is pointless. Does that ageing apartment block below Calvary still exist? The passage with the battered walls, the lift that grumbles and moans, the plain brown door with the doorbell the initiated ring three times, the clutter on the landing? Are footsteps still heard when the doorbell rings? Is there still the red carpet that Lizzie peed on a hundred times — and Tommie too, no doubt? And the row of shoes and slippers, the coatrack with the red-striped cloth that I made years and years ago? And the mirror that showed us getting old and the boys getting bigger? I can't see myself in it. The mirror is blank.

I know it all exists, but as the Solipsists say: If I can't perceive it, what bloody use is this awareness?

Just beyond the door, is there still the bathroom where I could shave with hot water? To look in the mirror and not hurry, to shave myself slowly and thoroughly the way men do who are calm and even-tempered? Is there a bathtub in that bathroom that you can run hot water into and then submerge yourself in? The water is hot. Air is released from the pores of my thighs and forms little beads. The bath could be a bit bigger so that I could stretch out fully and have only my head emerge from the water. I have to bend my knees — it's better that way because only my knees are left out of the water and the heat penetrates my chest and spreads over my shoulders and back. Finally a sponge behind my head to soften the edge of the bath and now it starts to be blissful. I feel like falling asleep for a few moments at least and pass from languor to insensibility. To open a vein and bleed to death like the Roman Stoics when they received a telegram from the emperor telling them they get on his nerves and that Rome has too many intellectuals.

Is there such a thing as a clean shirt that doesn't stink? One that's ironed soft and has buttons that fasten at the cuffs and the neck? It doesn't have to be white, an ordinary flannel one will do — I'm not going anywhere, after all. I still have to make the dinner. The meat lies on a white plate. Are there still plates? And I take a knife and sharpen it. There must be knives still. The knife slices into the onion and suddenly there is a snow-white pile waiting to sizzle in the hot oil. That blue miracle is burning gas. The pepper is green and the tomatoes red. And the spices were brought from all over the world. The yellowish curry powder from India. And the radio drones news about that silly world. All I have to do is turn the knob and I can have someone talking German, English, or even French — I have a chance to find out if my pronunciation is right when I say "Je ne vous entends pas du tout." Is it still there? I know it is, but there is a slight doubt, though.

And what about my writing desk? Is that still there? And the typewriter? You tap a few keys and you have a whole word. At the end of the row it rings. Just one more sentence and it'll be the end of the page and I can take it out of the machine and lay it to one side. Ostensibly nothing has happened, but maybe on that page there is something that will make someone happy. Some thought, some surprising message, or an expression of love. It has to be an aberration of civilization that an ordinary typewriter can be a source of delight, but it was an aberration I suffered from. I would lay aside each page with the same feeling as laying aside an axe after chopping a pile of firewood. Not always, though. Sometimes I felt there was no point in chopping that paper-wood that wouldn't even heat a room. But often I would forget about it and caress the typed page with my eyes, as if it were a painting I'd made a particularly good job of. Is it still there?

But do you know what, my love? We'll go outside and see if it still exists. Never mind the sleet, we need a change of air. What about the crossroads — are the roadworks completed? People use the footbridge to cross the road, leaving the cars beneath them to splash each other. Is it still there? It's cold, so I suggest we go to the Šenckvická viecha tavern to get warm. There's nothing attractive about it. Drunken soldiers, drink-splashed tables. But we'll have a lokša and a glass of burčák.[12] We're just

12. Lokša: a pastry of potato dough; burčák: new wine.

ordinary people here and generally talk just like everyone else. I can actually hear what they're saying — nobody has any secrets. I'll have another glass. You mustn't, because it's sweet. Maybe Milan and Marta will come. Marta will sit down next to me, like a little bird. And from the way she looks at Milan it's obvious she's in love with him. No man can look with love the way a woman can. The sort of gaze that is immediately noticeable. Men gaze with affection, satisfaction, admiration, anxiousness, confusion, and all sorts of other things. But I've never seen a man gaze with love. Or maybe I'm unable to recognize it in a man. But I notice it with women. And I could tell some of those amusing anecdotes about Milan when he was small. The only way to feel right is at every moment to suppress our sceptical detachment from reality, so that every word is the whole truth and all our wishes come true. Oh no, they don't! Is it still possible to walk down Pražská Street and round by Alma's and then as far as that crazy square that isn't for people, just for the traffic? Does Šenckvická still exist? Yes, I know it does, but . . .

11.15.81

It's an icy cold Sunday again like last week. Snow lies on the roofs outside. So I'll ask about something warm.

Is there still the great big stove in the middle of the room at Miro's?[13] Whenever I place my hands on it I can feel the warmth transfer to them from the bricks. Is there still the picture of the little red-roofed cottages and the leaping game, and the little colored lights in the aquaria with the fish swimming back and forth. And homemade wine on the table with little corn cobs and homemade sausage? And a conversation about something else — sentences that have a beginning and an end, with all sorts of colorful words that I haven't heard in a long time — stories about interesting people. Or talk about something abstract and fatuous, that has nothing to do with prison, money, or the law. The afterlife, for

13. The Bratislava home of the philosopher Miroslav Kusý and his family.

instance, when it is as if you are moving along a tunnel towards the light, towards some calm, quiet glow where you meet your ancestors. Are there still silly conversations about books, about some girl crying because she couldn't read a particular book? What is beautiful? Beautiful is what is dreamed up and written down on paper. But not only that. What is beautiful is a little child coming out of the bathroom in its pyjamas, all fragrant, and saying, "Night, night, Uncle Milan," and giving me a kiss and knowing nothing about people and maybe even thinking that they are all good. Is there such a thing as hailing a taxi on the street late on a Friday night? Inside it's warm and there is music playing and we don't have to get up in the morning. Of course, it all exists, but nevertheless I do have a shadow of a doubt.

Is there still the cinema at Veľké Karlovice where it is so warm inside and we are all on our own? They are showing a Hungarian film and nobody wants to tear themselves away from the television. Is there still the path with the frozen snow, the deserted ski run with the ski-tow poles, the snow-covered chalets with lights on inside as people are sitting there in the warmth? Why shouldn't it exist?

And is there still the Brno road? I mean the old road, not the highway. And the boys sitting behind me and playing the fool. On the way back they'll sit in front and press the accelerator. Unloading all our clutter at the quarry and dragging it all upstairs, and then Granddad saying welcome and Grandma shouting "Oh my God — Eva," though she's known we're coming for ages. And you're already nervy because the hand basin in the bathroom is all mucky. But I'll breathe in that mixture of apples and mold and look forward to the evening when I'll hear the murmur of the boys in the attic. Maybe there are mushrooms growing Tišnov way. Well, those are things that don't exist any more. For you now there are trips to Prague. Maybe they have something going for them, such as how much I look forward to them. And now you're familiar with the prison entrance, which I've already forgotten. Then the moment of agitation until I appear in the doorway, trembling and staring at you as at an apparition. That exists, and thank God for that, at least. Maybe one day you'll look back on it as something beautiful, driving all that way and not talking much, just watching the kilometers fly by. Here's the turn-off for Jelenov where there could be a red-hot sawdust stove, and just beyond the window a forest with conifer scent and pictures of the Virgin. And when even that will exist no more it will be part of our souls.

I know that there exists plenty of warmth in this world. Such as that pool at Slovnaft that I visited one morning with Petr and Milan: its surface was smooth and reflected the sun. Everything was fed with some remote energy. And Milan is swimming to the bottom and I can see him as if behind glass, like a naked astronaut in a free-fall chamber. A mere hour of happiness. An hour because I can see a big clock. There are all sorts of clocks wherever you look and they measure out the time for warmth and happiness. Even the ordinary alarm clock on the side table in the living room. What about the padded overalls I wore when I was on the concrete mixer — do they still exist? I used to stride to lunch in them and the cold wind never bothered me. And poor old Zora would gambol around me like a lunatic, happy that we were alone together. I could think in the wind while walking briskly along; and I could stop somewhere, and almost everywhere I'd be welcomed with a glass. The one element of this that no longer exists is Zora, the only dog in my whole life who loved me.

I almost forgot to ask whether television still exists — those moving pictures. "Die Sprecherin Maria Eva Klinger."[14] But there's one thing that certainly doesn't exist any more: the AKH affair.[15] Likewise, there is no longer any football or hockey or the comments we would trade about a fine attack or a good shot, even when it missed. It can't exist any more because Petr's not there and, like you, Milan despises TV sport. But why do I even mention it, seeing that I don't miss it. But all the same I'd like to hear what Portisch or Lengyel[16] say about it. It would bother

14. Maria Eva Klinger: announcer on the Vienna II TV station that could be received in Bratislava.
15. AKH affair: a case of embezzlement involving the Austrian Allgemeine Krankenhaus (AKH) that was widely reported by Vienna II.
16. Presenters on "Klub Zwei," a popular Austrian current affairs program.

me a lot more if there ceased to exist the bus that stops in front of our house and brings you home when I've been indoors on my own for more than two hours. Those paltry two hours compared to the months that have gone by during which no buses ran. I know for certain that as soon as the bus has driven off and cleared the view you will look up at the window. And I will step behind the curtain, because I'm ashamed of looking at you from the window, after all these years; and all the time I realize that you will see footprints in the carpet anyway, and it will be more powerful than the fact I've been waiting for you by the window with the curtains drawn. The buses still run, both ours and the Hungarians'. But for you now the only person who will get off will be Milan, and that doesn't happen often because he has always made sure that his life has no rules, and that also applies to regular comings and goings.

I am in doubts about the existence of people I'm fond of. They ring the bell and I'm glad to see them. Sometimes I have something to offer them by way of refreshment, sometimes not. They sit in the kitchen or in an armchair and I observe them as I listen to their ideas or stories and am glad there are people like that in the world. I like best of all those who tell me something I've never heard about before, or tell me about other people, or the things they've experienced, and I relish life's richness. Maybe they are sitting in the armchair at this very moment but I, alas, can't hear what the conversation is about. I won't name them.

There is only one of those I loved who won't be coming. My old uncle. Almost always the same and never ageing, and then suddenly dead. He knew that his life was slowly coming to an end and he talked about it almost without regret. Goodness knows how he took his death. It always struck me that for many years he participated in life as an observer. Therein lay his wisdom. He accumulated so much experience in the course of his life that he perceived everything around him as a re-run of things that had already happened. He had already received answers to all his questions and modern history didn't interest him. He knew that people always repeated "denselben Quatsch."[17] If I'd been brave enough,

17. Denselben Quatsch: The same old garbage.

I'd have told him I didn't approve of his premature stoicism. I always regretted that a man of his stature should withdraw so soon from the world and only observe it from a distance. He was a greater man than many who run their countries' affairs. But I understood him. He had explored life's values and opted for the simplest. And he knew so much. But he was like a private library, accessible only to his intimates, of whom I am happy to have been one. He once told me that he was only writing poems now. I'd love to read them. Maybe one of his sons could copy them out. They are sure to be wise, and maybe beautiful, too.

That's something else that no longer exists: those late afternoons, a bottle of red Frankovka, cigarette ash, and that curious bilingual torrent of words. The most beautiful thing about them was that they never concealed his enjoyment of those meetings, and I hope we didn't conceal our fondness for him or our affinity with him. And as I write this I am downcast, because I don't need to ask, I simply know that such meetings are a thing of the past and all that remains is an indelible impression in the minds of those who sat around that little table with the red wine. I was terribly aware of his frailty each time we embraced on parting. He would leave feeling uncertain of our next meeting. I could sense it, and he wasn't someone who needed false reassurance. A firm handshake sufficed. Perhaps he realized how much I understood him.

And yet I really do know that many of life's beautiful aspects exist. As I once wrote, I try with all my heart not to envy anyone. On the contrary, I feel like shouting all the time: cherish them, you fools! But I'm sure there's nothing sinful about regretting those delights of life. It is regret tinged with a sweet frisson — everything is played out in the memory, but somehow lacks color and taste; my senses are paralyzed from being so long deprived of light, colors, scents, sounds, tastes, and warmth.

11.16.81

There are a thousand things I could ask about in this way. Maybe there are five thousand things that really matter to me — or maybe only five.

And they are all sensory experiences connected with some special moment when the four of us were together. Such as four o'clock on a cold, misty, and drizzly morning when Lizzie returned and leaped from that pile of planks right into your arms. That's us: stupid with sleep and in a certain sense deranged in the fuss we made about an errant cat, aware in the back of our minds that it is not an animal but a reincarnated soul as that marvelous Indian with the splendid Sikh turban said with a gentle smile. Something always exists in the world of humans. So I'd better not even ask. Or I'll just ask whether there is still the coil in our little electric heater that glows red in the dark. It radiates heat into bare feet. They are my legs, and I'm waiting for you to come home. Shadows are thrown onto the window blinds like onto the walls of Plato's cave. The blue glow of the fluorescent street lighting. By now cars are few and far between, it's mostly night taxis. Or I overhear the idiotic mumbling of the loudspeakers at the railway station. It's not even background any more but part of life. And by now I don't even want it to be otherwise. That red-glowing coil has already determined everything. It's a mystery and I'm too lethargic to interpret its message. I simply accept it, without fully understanding it. In the same way I accept the opening of the door, the touch of crepe pyjamas, and the scent of soap and toothpaste. And likewise I accept breath and the taste of saliva and the touches that involve every particle of the body. That mystery incorporates other happenings: far-off lovemaking on a meadow beneath a night sky, various silent moments outside the windows of chalets and hotels, a sort of distant moon moving along the curtains, and for the life of me I can't remember where it was. Everything centered on that red-hot coil, and I don't want it explained.

Except that I can ask whether it exists also. After all, this is my mystery and accessible to my senses alone. Maybe that backdrop exists. Maybe the coil glows red hot and some voice announces the train departures. But all I hear is the sound of airplanes roaring down the runway and my eyes are fixed on a single bare bulb. So I give up trying to decide what exists and what doesn't. But even so, I enjoyed writing it and I was so immersed in writing it that I didn't see or hear a thing. Deaf and blind,

I saw and heard my inner self.

2.6.82

I'm fully aware how irksome my birthday always was. It was hard to please me. However hard I tried, I never managed to work up a proper appreciation of things bought for money. I much preferred happenings and encounters: when Ila[18] came on a visit or when Milan and Marta came to see me. I loved the gathering for my fiftieth, for instance. I derive a certain enjoyment from the melancholy that seizes you unawares when you happen to count the years that have passed. I'm sure I'll enjoy that melancholy this year, too. And I won't have to hide it from anyone. And since, my love, we grow wiser as we grow older, I shouldn't think it'll be anything to match the despair you were plunged into on your thirtieth birthday so intensely that you were ready to hang yourself from the apple tree, almost like Sergei Yesenin.[19] What a glorious night that was!

Survivors recall that it gave everyone enormous pleasure when I was born. I expect so, because Fredo and Ila were already big and I came along as something to be spoiled and played with. Only Ila was fed up because she was harnessed to the carriage. I must have had a beautiful childhood because I can't recall a single injustice done to me by those around me. All I remember is that everyone showered me with love and attention. I can recall fairly well the selfish pleasure I derived from the commotion that reigned any time I came down with some silly flu or other. How they would start heating the room like mad with the high tiled stove, which gave off a fragrant warmth that no one knows nowadays. Every Sunday I would creep into Mom and Dad's bed. They used to sleep in a sort of reddish feather bed and must still have been very young — heavens, they can't have been much over thirty! A pity I can't see them with the eyes I have now. All I can remember is Mommy crying "Ouch,

18. Ila: Šimečka's sister Ilona (b. 1921).

19. Sergei Aleksandrovich Yesenin: 1895–1925, Russian poet. Disillusionment with the Russian Revolution, his failed marriages, and alcoholism contributed to his suicide.

ouch" when I crawled over her. It's very possible that they smacked me from time to time, but I don't recall it. I quiver with happiness these days whenever I recall what a good time I had. Mother would put a great big pot on the stove to heat water and pour it into a big wooden tub. And then she'd scrub me with a white cake of Shicts' soap with the stag on it. I can still feel her hands on my face and the sting of the soap in my eyes. You boys have never enjoyed that primitive enjoyment under the shower. Yes, and the packets of soap used to contain oblong pictures of locomotives.

It strikes me that the quality of the generations has declined since mothers have ceased to be at home with their children. I'm sure it's a very conservative view, but I dare to voice it in private. Otherwise, how could my mother have looked after me like that? And apart from that she kept chickens, and I can still hear her calling "pipipipipi" to them and throwing them grain. Or she would force-feed maize to the goose and I was allowed to watch. She would also make it swallow a ten-heller coin and I would get it as a present when the goose was slaughtered. It would be smooth and shine like gold. My mother had plenty of time to take care of me. Dad worked for us, and we would go and peep through a hole in the wicker fence into the factory where he'd be sitting importantly at his desk. That was when Mother would take me shopping with her to the Co-op shop. She would have a chat in the shop and in return I would get a roll with butter and ham. It cost 50 hellers and Mother would pay the money with a sigh. But that was something so good that now I'll have to go and spit into the latrine, because the very thought of it makes my mouth water so much. I expect I ought to have written "origin: bourgeois" on forms, because how many kids in those days would have gotten a ham roll from their mother?

It's a matter of eternal regret, boys, that I was never able to show you that little settlement inside the factory where we used to live. It really was heaven on earth. A "small primitive community." Or at least that is what it was for us children. There could have been fifty of them and they were all my pals. I was welcome in all their homes. One lady I used to visit had a big green parrot in a cage. One birthday I was given a scooter and that made me really big: I was king of the world, like Cassius Clay. And so, like Citizen Kane, I've never been as happy with a birthday since. That could have been March 6, 1937. That just goes to show — and at that moment the world stood on the verge of catastrophe.

2.7.82

See how engrossed I became. It quite often happens that I can't help myself getting wrapped up in childhood memories and unable to tear myself away from the subject. It's probably a natural compensation for the pitiful present circumstances — the deprivation, cold, and emptiness — that one gets drawn back to the marvelous sub-tropical zone of years long departed. By now I feel a bit like Božena Němcová[20] with her Sultan and Tyrel, because I lived with dogs too: Bobby and Pete. Bobby was black and Pete was white with brown patches. You were not allowed to take Bobby's bone when he was gnawing it under the couch. Once he bit my finger. Pete was a puppy and we messed around together quite a bit.

It simply looks as if I use my birthday to recall old times. If ever I get around to writing my memoirs, I'll stop at my tenth birthday. And it will make splendid reading.

There you are, I recall getting a scooter for some birthday in my childhood. Then I remember getting a Swiss watch from Ila for my fifteenth birthday . . . no, it was already my sixteenth. And I don't remember my twentieth, my twenty-fifth, my thirtieth, or my thirty-fifth. On my fortieth birthday I received my dismissal notice. That I do remember. I told the bursar that it was a bit unfortunate, and the poor fellow said he'd willingly change the date, but I told him it didn't matter any more. So my dismissal notice really does bear the date of March 6, 1970.

My fiftieth birthday is still so recent I'll have to recall it. Such as the

---

20. Božena Němcová: 1820-1862, one of the best-known Czech writers of the 19th century, famous for her recollections of her childhood, particularly *The Grandmother.*

moment when that insolent waiter at Peklo refused to serve us a drink. It was just as well, as the cops were already waiting for us. And so it strikes me that it was all symptomatic and just a little hint that my future birthdays wouldn't be worth a light. Above all the ones still to come. Just think how easy it would be for you to think up something that would give me really great pleasure. For instance, you, Muki, could bring me a roll and butter on a plate and a cup of fragrant tea. And on top of that two hours of conversation and cuddling and a half-hour of quiet sipping with our legs stretched out towards the radiant heater. I don't know whether I'd survive such a profusion of gifts. Milan would also give me a couple of hours — my demands are moderate. I'd stretch out on the couch and he would read me something he'd written. Meanwhile he'd put something quiet on the record player for me. Then he'd have to go back to Marta. Petr would then take over and tell me about life in uniform. And again I'd need to have some music to listen to. We could also talk about the universe for a while. That's about all I could take without cracking beneath the weight of that happiness. And it wouldn't cost you a penny. How simple it is. In the future I won't accept any other gifts for my birthday.

Sometimes I wonder who actually prevents you giving me gifts like those? I try in vain to pin the blame on someone. But however much I rack my brains I keep on coming back to Kafka's old tune. Quite simply, they came for me and now I'll stand trial. I was quite envious of those of my fellow-prisoners who were able to define precisely what brought them here. They spent a lot of time analyzing in detail where they slipped up. And they railed in magnificent hatred against their treacherous accomplices and others whom they regarded as the cause of their misfortune. I alone sit here in an absurd world without cause and effect. When I try to discover where it all began, I travel back through history bit by bit until I find myself in distant centuries. And all the time I observe the same causes and effects. The constant imprisonment of the spirit in a history of stupidities, intolerance, and cruelty. So I can't even choose. There isn't one bit of history in which universal respect, tolerance, and respect for human dignity might last the space of even a short human life. In fact, I can't even recall such a life story of happiness and peace. Such life stories probably weren't worth it, so we know nothing of them. Whoever lived in the reign of Charles IV[21] had nothing to complain about. But those who made it into Wenceslas' reign[22] cried over their earnings. In Rudolf II's time[23] only the alchemists and astrologers were well off. I read in Zikmund Winter[24] about the troubles they encountered with the censor when they tried to put on a play about Oldřich and Božena.[25] Quite simply they were banned from putting it on, and by then they actually had tickets already printed. To tell you the truth, I would be best off under Metternich[26] and Bach[27]. Namely, the fantastic nineteenth century. Someone like Palacký[28] was immune. I expect that it wasn't half as bad in Brixen as it was here, but Havliček[29] really did write dreadful things. I managed to get a selection of his articles to read here. I wouldn't have had his courage. He was terribly anti-German. Yet he understood the period he lived in better than anyone else. But everything in that century seems so wonderfully idyllic to me. In Vienna, the students stormed the prime minister's palace and he came out and argued with them even though they patently represented no one but themselves and their own crazy revolutionary consciousness.

But all the horrors of the twentieth century make me quite ill. On two

---

21. Charles IV: 1316–78, Holy Roman Emperor (1355–78); succeeded his father, John of Luxemburg, as King of Bohemia (1346).
22. Wenceslas: 1361–1419, Holy Roman Emperor (uncrowned) and German king (1378–1400), King of Bohemia (1378–1419) as Wenceslas IV, Elector of Brandenburg (1373–76); son and successor of Emperor Charles IV.
23. Rudolf II: Holy Roman Emperor and King of Bohemia (1576–1612).
24. Zikmund Winter: 1846-1912, Czech historian and writer who chiefly dealt with the 15th-17th centuries.
25. Oldřich: prince who ruled the Czech lands 1012-1034; Božena: his abducted wife.
26. Metternich, Clemens Wenzel Nepomuk Lothar, Fürst von: 1773–1859, Austrian statesman. His system depended on censorship, espionage, and the suppression of revolutionary and nationalist movements.
27. Alexander Bach: 1813–93, Austrian politician. As minister of the interior (1849–59) he instituted the Bach system for the centralization and Germanization of Habsburg lands.
28. František Palacký: 1798-1876. Czech historian who was active as a spokesman of Czech political and cultural interests. Known as the "Father of the Nation."
29. Karel Borovský Havliček: 1821-1856, Czech journalist and satirical poet. An opponent of absolutism and ecclesiastical authority, he was exiled to Brixen in the South Tyrol in 1851.

occasions, for instance, I managed to get books by Vančura[30] to read. That language of his thrilled me and I'd roll his sentences around on my tongue. As I have time enough to spare, I would read slowly like a schoolboy. It struck me that there could have been no kinder or wiser person living at that time. I have a feeling he was detained here at the Ruzyně barracks, which I can see from my window. And then they killed him. I wonder whether the Germans knew who they were killing. They had probably never read Vančura or it seemed to them like some Czech *Barbarei*. So he stood there, neither his judges nor his executioners knowing a thing about him. They simply dispatched him along with the rest. I wonder what he felt. Could he have suspected that in forty years time someone on the same historical spot would read his books and think about him so intensely, as if summoning him from the grave? Maybe he'd have died more easy in his mind had he known it for sure. And he could have known, because that's the way it always is, and I fear it always will be.

I have no doubts even about that fateful year of nineteen eighty-four. To tell the truth, I find it hard not to identify with Winston.[31] I know that literary figure almost by heart and his words come to mind by day and night, and sometimes I get the feeling they prevent me from thinking my own thoughts. Whenever I read the newspaper I can't help trying to discover what has been changed and which worthy comrade has decided to amend reality according to the latest official speech. Unlike Winston, who was devastated about knowing nothing in particular about the past, I am devastated by the fact I know so much. Sometimes I would actually welcome a general brainwashing, so that I wouldn't have to think about the fact that the chocolate ration was supposed to be raised, not lowered, and that a few years ago Eurasia was waging war with Oceania, not Eastasia. In other words, what bothers me is not that I know little about the past, but that I know too much; it literally makes me sick to

30. Vladislav Vančura: 1891-1942, Czech writer who experimented with language and form. A non-doctrinaire Communist, he was executed by the Nazis.
31. Winston Smith: the protagonist of George Orwell's anti-utopian novel *Nineteen Eighty-Four* (translated into Czech by Eva Šimečková).

see how intensively they are working at the Minitru.[32] In fact, everything has happened on account of my memory and my inability to forget things as they really were, as well as our old and frayed dreams and ideals. I simply couldn't master the damned Doublethink method. To be frank, I wouldn't mind experiencing it at least once to know what it feels like in one's head. But most frequently I recall that scene with Julia when they're standing at the window above that antiquarian shop and suddenly they say, "We are dead." I strive to understand what it all means and how believable or otherwise that sentence is. I simply don't think it is by accident that I have spent so much time with that Winston. It's as if our destinies somehow coincided. And even now, when you arrive here on a visit after a long interval, I suddenly realize we are drinking real coffee. Most of all I struggle with that green water into which everything sinks. I don't want to admit the possibility that it could happen, though I suspect that it is. After all, you know too that our lives are divided and that we are sinking, aware all the while that the water is beginning to cover the features we know so well. I must look different to you in my changed guise. I had to let them pull another of my front teeth.

2.8.82

I'll be fifty-two, and all of a sudden I have the feeling that I already know everything substantial there is to know about life and nothing surprising is going to happen inside me either. Real thirst for life that consists essentially of curiosity about the changes in one's own existence is gradually evaporating from me. Naturally there remains an extrovert curiosity that is related to the world. But even that is something I experience more as the curiosity of a spectator. It is a theatre of sorts, but I increasingly have the impression that I know the play or I've read it at least and know basically what it's about, as you always do when you go to a performance of Shakespeare. So I'm more curious about how the actors will perform

32. The Ministry of Truth in *Nineteen Eighty-Four.*

their roles, whether it will be hammed up or a great production that will move us or make us laugh.

But maybe I'm wrong and the real thirst for life is merely slumbering in the monotony of the days here, which has a hypnotic effect similar to the regular dripping of water or the ticking of a clock. It would be fine if I were mistaken. The trouble is that even if I'm wrong it will have no effect on the depth of the green water that we're sinking into. And there's nothing we can do about it. Perhaps merely to try to remember it all.

So what else can you do about my birthday? Just spend it like any other day. I know that you think about me a lot and I shouldn't think you'll have to force yourselves to think about me more on that particular day. And in fact we ought to drop it all and accept that there is no such thing as important days designated in advance. A consciousness bound by various anniversaries is a false consciousness. The value of days is not determined by their present historical significance but by their actual content. That's the way we have to look at it, and I'm an idiot for having started with this birthday business in the first place. This sort of thinking merely wears me down with slushy sentiment and is totally pointless. Away with it!

2.18.1982

Just to be on the safe side, I'll address this letter to Brno, even though I've received the gratifying news that the letters I wrote back in November have reached home. The most reliable way is to send them to you, Grandma.[33] I worked this out today when I received a packet that they sent me with a letter scarcely three weeks ago: this means that you must have received my letter within about two weeks, which is a world record for our correspondence so far. I don't need to tell you how pleased and heartened I am.

33. Šimečka's mother-in-law.

Marta, I can't thank you enough for all the things you put in the package. I expect the girls made the apple dolly. Thank you so much for the apples, oranges, cigarettes, honey, and salami. And most of all, what a fantastic idea it was to send me those cress seeds. I immediately planted them on some damp cotton wool and I can't wait to see what will grow out of them. Maybe those herbs will give me as much pleasure as spring, which will soon be making little green shoots appear outside. I will take loving care of these little plants and observe them as they grow. If they really are edible, then I will eat them with relish (though I don't know if I will have the heart to). I've also attached your apple dolly to the good luck wheel left over from Christmas that has already brought me luck in that you receive my letters and I am blessed with yours. The good luck wheel and the dolly are attached to the sheet of paper where I write Italian proverbs,[34] in order to have them in front of my eyes all the time and never forget them. They include such things as: He who does no ill need have no fear (*Mal non fare, panza non avere*), which is one I especially like as it illustrates the age-old false belief in human goodness. Another one I've written is about the early bird catching the worm (*Le ore della mattina hanno il oro in bocca*) — literally: the morning hours have gold in their mouths. I also find this a gratifying piece of wisdom. I'm up like a lark at six a.m., but the only worm I catch is another night in this cell. There is nothing for it but to cling to the sceptical *non si se mai* — one never knows. Maybe I'll hop one day to the garden at Bystrc,[35] peck at a raspberry here, a blackcurrant there and then have a go at the cherries. You'll be there too and won't even realize that the early bird is me.

It's a week since I received your letters and I'm all aquiver again at the thought that there might be . . . But I'd better not build up my hopes in case I'm disappointed. Over these past nine months I've taught myself to tear all hopes mercilessly out of my heart, because they have been dashed so often that the fragments are piling up and will end up overwhelming me. So every morning I get up and say to myself: No, there's

34. Šimečka was teaching himself Italian.
35. Bystrc: the suburb of Brno where his parents-in-law lived.

no chance of receiving any letters today; it's too soon; no, there can't be any today, they've never come on a Thursday yet, only on Fridays, Wednesdays, and Tuesdays. So I start my day without any hope, and all of a sudden there you are: a packet of Danish cress seeds. And straight away life is full of hope that my cress will sprout and turn green. Life is full of surprises.

Milan, I'll continue with our dialogue about your letters as I promised. I can feel right through the overalls I'm wearing and through my very skin your yearning to put this entire muddled world to rights and steer your thoughts into a clear space. And it strikes me that you're increasingly moving away from a simple vision of things towards deciphering their mysterious inner substance. You read philosophers and you yourself are one; I can tell by the way you frame questions. You know full well that I don't have a particularly high opinion of philosophy, especially of the academic variety. Well, so far there's no risk of your encountering it. You're lucky. After all, it's much better to read Kant just for the sake of it, as a spiritual exercise. It's probably more useful and entertaining than watching TV.

I'm reading the first lines of your letter from January 6, Milan, where you write about how there is suddenly a deeper public awareness of uncertainty and a sense that probably nothing will stay as it is. You know, of course, that we discussed it years ago and there weren't many people ready to believe it. If I disregard all secondary considerations (which aren't really secondary in the proper sense of the word), it strikes me that what we and the whole world are experiencing is a profound sense of crisis of the European (or "white") concept of civilization. (After all, there isn't any other; all nations have accepted this concept in this century — just look at the Japanese and Chinese.) The concept came into being back in the 19th century and its fairy godmothers were two great ideals: on the one hand, scientific, technical, and industrial progress; and on the other, the universal belief in a social revolution that was supposed to create a just, free, and more-or-less egalitarian order. That has all been written about. The first ideal went on being nourished by new sap. It flowered unceasingly: all of Verne's visions were fulfilled, and even bolder ones. No heed was paid to any warnings. In fact it was not until quite recently that the idea of progress received a jolt with the energy crisis, ecological concerns, and the scaling down of grandiose schemes. When I was your age I once acted as a guide at a sort of exhibition about the future. In some future era (which, according to the forecasts of those days is already behind us) automated electric tractors would plow huge fields yielding three-eared corn, deserts would be surrounded by windbreaks, and people would sing for sheer joy. Who would have thought that one day they'd be rummaging in trash cans for old bread for their pigs. In the early sixties, Americans were booking tickets for trips to Mars and Venus. The never-ending Verne story. You won't remember it, but we actually gave you a bath in the Danube. Nobody ever thought that in twenty years that river would become a stinking sewer. What is remarkable is that nowadays everyone is thoroughly familiar with those dashed hopes. Not, of course, because the tickets to Mars or even to the Moon have expired, but above all because the price of gas and the Sunday roast have gone up, and because that footprint that Armstrong left on the Moon will probably be the only one for a long time to come. That's the hopeful element. Because nothing boosted consumers' don't-care attitudes as much as that secular faith in the incessant growth of GNP. Only in the context of that faith could the concept of endlessly increasing affluence become the guiding idea of the planet. But all this is patently obvious and there is little point in dwelling on it at length. This faith is eroded every day by hundreds of minor defects in that affluence. After all, even governments are trying to counteract that optimism, in spite of the fact that a mere decade ago they were propagating it with all means at their disposal.

2.19.82

However, I was always more interested in the failures of that other great ideal: the speedy establishment of an order of justice and even affluence.

Maybe it was an inkling of the fateful significance of that lunatic belief that induced me to start studying utopias then. But I don't maintain that I already knew how deeply this century would be marked by the crumbling of utopian beliefs. I enjoyed tracing the growth of some vague yearning for "order" and all the enthusiasm that was unleashed when it was assisted by industry, technology, science, the working class, and every new and unprecedented phenomenon. It was the time when utopias became scientific and old doubts about the "inflexibility" of the human material were jettisoned. It started in the middle of the last century and lasted a hundred years, or maybe even a bit longer. The first evidence of disillusionment in that belief manifested itself at the end of the 1950s. Up till then, certain things could only be explained from outside. At that moment it started to become clear that the explanation had to come from inside.

I'm sure I don't have to describe to you in detail how that disillusionment grew chiefly out of criticism of the social realities in the countries that declared themselves to be the fulfilment of those old hopes. For a long time all they had to do was compare what had gone before with what had developed. This was largely inconclusive as far as the system's effectiveness was concerned, because the growth of production was almost entirely related to technological progress, and that applied to the entire planet. The cardinal issue remained how this social reality compared with the original hopes, because it was this correlation that was to determine whether the concept of European civilization was well founded. In this connection, it is largely immaterial whether we have more automatic washing machines than we had fifty years ago, when there were none. Looking back over those hundred years, the only important thing is if an order was created — or the basis of an order, at least — that would correspond to those original hopes. One important reason for the uncertainty and the catastrophic awareness of the present day, though not the main one, is the knowledge that it did not happen. It happened neither in terms of the economic premises nor, which is worse, in terms of the social premises — and here I have in mind the assumptions of social harmony that were part of those hopes. It didn't happen, even though steps could have been taken in that direction, which would have cost little and had no effect on the state of affluence. Inadequate economic development tended to be used as an excuse rather than as a convincing argument. Even in a poor community it is possible to lay the basis for social harmony — more easily, in fact, than in a rich one.

The second disillusionment has naturally given rise to widespread debate. This is because of ideological inertia. This controversy could run on for another century, because it has long since lacked any precise criteria for assessing it. One would have to go back to the very beginning, to the source of those hopes. A hundred-year-old face can't be assessed in terms of how it looked ten years ago, as the difference in decrepitude is not particularly great. But if we compare it with the youthful face of those ideals, with its ardent gaze and scarlet lips, or with how it looked at the dawn of the day when the *Aurora*'s guns rang out, then we see it in due proportion. This senility doesn't only relate to Eastern Europe, it relates to the entire planet.

You see, a virtually universal political and social objective has been established throughout the world: prosperity combined with social justice and social welfare. (Just notice how the isolated national concepts based on old-style nationalism have died out over the recent decades; nationalism only comes into existence where there is a widespread feeling that another nation is preventing the attainment of some common goal. Polish nationalism is also only an expression of that feeling.)

But I'm not particularly concerned here with proof. The best proof is the general feeling that you described in your letter. Because in the final analysis, social events are determined by those mass feelings and not by specialized discussions between teams of propaganda experts. Those can be easily organized. So if we leave to one side the business of proof that that world is at present concerned with and which gave rise to the polemic between the Soviet and Italian Communists, the outstanding question remains: What now? The concept of European civilization based on the two-hundred-year-old hopes already mentioned is slowly being extinguished. And as we examine the ideological goods on offer — now and in recent years — we discover that there is no available alternative with the scope or ability to control the active section of people. And it's unlikely that there ever will be, because it is inappropriate for this world — or put another way: there is no mass market for it. In view of the present level of material existence in Europe and most of the industrialized countries, there is nothing for an effective ideological concept to grow out of, because in the past it was always the product of social desperation. I don't think this is any misfortune, though. On the contrary, it is a major plus of the present situation. The relatively non-ideological space that is coming into existence is favorable for an assessment of the entire ideological legacy of the past and a general stocktaking and spring-cleaning. Best of all, it will mean a shift away from the amorphous ideology of affluence which has dominated European civilization. Naturally, people won't abandon their concept of affluence, but the present crisis will be a short, sharp lesson. Because henceforth the question will be: Affluence? Yes, but at what price? Maybe the qualified majority will start to decide the price it's not prepared to pay. Such as the destruction of nature, the decline of intellectual culture, jeopardizing the future, etc. That is certainly nothing to regret. Maybe a way will actually be found of extending affluence by gradually abandoning social selfishness and wasteful luxury. The first signs of that trend are already visible and perhaps it will actually catch people's imaginations. In a new situation, various existing projects for a more intensive lifestyle and group living, as well as old and new idealisms, all sorts of experiments in social relationships, could come into their own. There is no need to think up anything new in this respect. Quite simply, it can only be to the good to break free of illusions about constantly increasing affluence. (Unless, of course, economic incompetence brings the world to the brink of starvation and ushers in the last battle for a crust of bread. But that doesn't look likely.)

3.26.82

Yesterday was March 25: another detention period completed. During the evening I wondered whether you were standing once more at the window waiting for the express from Prague, and I was so sorry for you, my love, that I was a long time getting to sleep. Of course the remand extension notice didn't reach me in due time. I couldn't care less about it. It has always arrived as much as a week late. So in just a few days' time it will be a year. There was a time when a year like this was beyond my imagination and yours too, I'm sure, and yet it'll soon be behind us. And no one will ever give it back to us. It has simply melted into time, in the same way that Milan's letters in the snow have probably melted in the fierce spring sunshine. But they were just as real as that year. From now on it will be an indelible part of our lives. Sorry I didn't appear at the hole in the fence. It's not my fault, I'd love to have been there. I would have arrived carrying a handful of tiny cress leaves grown from the seeds you sent me. I would chop them up and sprinkle them onto a slice of bread and butter. We would eat the bread and rid ourselves of all evil. It would be a ritual to drive out the spell and we would be happy ever after. But it can't be helped — I'll have to eat the cress on my own on Sunday night.

3.27.82

Milan, I've spent the last few days with you in the Tatras and warmed myself a bit at your stove. It's the stove of you both, yours and Marta's. This is the first time you've written about her as your wife. It was no doubt partly because of the atmosphere of cooperation in the cottage: chopping wood, keeping the fire alight, and cooking. I'm sure you remember how poetically Domino wrote about it, when he told how love could only exist when the man cut the corn and the woman gathered it after him. Therein lies the intrinsic truth: keeping the fire burning and other primitive concerns about the essential things of life constitute the age-old tie between man and woman. That's what people should seek for most of all. It's almost totally lacking in urban civilization. And yet we go crazy over comforts that alienate us; the only thing that links men and women these days is goggling at the television. The two of you are bound to have felt that shared security, and perhaps you won't forget it. But while I'm on the subject of the security you found so appealing in that wilderness, forgive me for casting a tiny shade of doubt on your discovery. In the social context, security is a very deceptive concept. I sometimes get the feeling that it is the opposite of freedom. A sense of security is so appealing that people are sometimes prepared to take it in exchange for freedom, which is essentially insecure. Or at least there are people who calmly watch as freedom is sacrificed to security. In other words, they prefer other people to take care of their security. But this would be a lengthy debate. Otherwise, I got enormous enjoyment from your various experiences and believe that it did you good to spend hours just being aware of the snow, the forest, and the distant contours of the Low Tatras. After all, it's what we've already talked about in our letters: the salutary effect of making a stop; the unalloyed joy of still beauty and reality sharply perceived.

We envied him, didn't we, Petr? I'm now so familiar with your days that by now I could almost live them with you. I'm keeping my fingers only slightly crossed for you because I'm sure you'll come out of it all unscathed. And you'll even have something stashed away for the future. Whenever you need it, you'll simply dip into your archive and pull out something that will fit perfectly any situation you find yourself in. What's more, Mother will soon be able to hang up a tape measure on the door to measure you and the time you have left.

All your descriptions of the hierarchy from rookie upwards are much more detailed than the ones we got from Milan; they started me thinking about social machinery in general. After all, that model doesn't only apply to your microcosm. It would be worth investigating how it evolved, because it didn't exist in my days, at least not to that extent, with all those rituals and customs. But if I were to set about it I would fill pages with abstractions. I truly regret, my boy, that I can't have such detailed conversations with you about it all as I had with Milan. Because later it might all be stale. If we don't seize the moment when everything is still vivid, it is hopeless going back. So something always trickles through our fingers, all the time, and we don't even need to be in prison. Let's console ourselves with the thought that there will always be something alive to engage our awareness.

I suppose it is part of life in this place that one often looks through the calendar and stops at dates connected with moments and turning-points in one's past. I am looking at just such a date now. On April 20, my brother would have celebrated his sixtieth birthday. I can imagine us all sitting around in that pleasant house at Zábřeh, and I'd be slapping my brother on the back and crossing swords with him the way we used to. And yet he's already many years dead. He vanished from our lives so suddenly that even now I find it hard to believe. I realize I've thought of him more often since I've been in here than in all the previous years. I'm not even sure why in prison my thoughts often turn to the dead. Maybe it's because I myself have a sense of suddenly disappearing from life. Maybe because I wonder about the meaning of closed lives as well and seek within my own life the meaning of everything that happens, both my everyday activities and precious moments of happiness, understanding, and insight. I also reflect on the strange mystery of kinship and what links me to people in the distant past whom I never actually knew and who lived their own special lives. Whatever else, I am their genetic descendant. I'd really love to know whether their world and everything they filled it with has any connection with my world, and whether some idea or feeling about life once wandered in their consciousness before finding me here in this cell at some hour of the night. Those people never wrote anything down — more's the pity! Or is it true that we are always something brand new and unique, which begins and ends with us? I know so dreadfully little about the people I come from!

Fredo was my brother in the same way, Petr, that you are Milan's and he yours. And yet I expect I knew infinitely less about him than you know about each other. Of course I knew his life story in detail, but what did I know about his inner life? Maybe I only imagined that it was a calm and happy one?

It was probably all because I was so much younger than my siblings. By the time I started to notice the world around me, Ila was already going to dance classes in a shiny green dress and Fredo was riding a splendid green bike. Yet I also remember them from the period when I shouldn't really remember them, because I should think they were still pushing me around in a carriage. But I remember a boy they used to call "a slacker" and recall how he'd get "a hiding," and he'd dance around Dad, who was wielding the whip that used to hang on the door, screaming and promising to do better at school. It was always on account of some dreadful nature study that probably no one finds dreadful nowadays. How old could I have been then? Four perhaps. My brother was at the receiving end of that age-old pedagogical method instead of me; I never recall being beaten. My siblings protected me, and at home I had a sense of total security — until, that is, everything changed, and security in Bohumín was sent packing by the war and Dad's death. My brother was a part of that familiar security, because it only took a look from my brother and any enemy of mine would creep away with his tail between his legs.

I remember him but he was always so much older. By the time I started school, he was already at the vocational school and was always drawing something with a marvelous black pencil. And when he got married I was still an unruly lad wondering what it all meant. I knew that he was going out with Zdenka and I don't think he ever went out with anyone else. I used to watch them curiously among the skaters at the rink, holding on to each other as they circled around. Zdenka fascinated me because she had natty ringlets all over her head like the actresses in German films. I expect it was the fashion. I reported on it at home, and Mother said that as he made his bed he'd have to lie in it. He made it well, and I enjoyed myself because there were schnitzels and pastries at the wedding reception, which were something unheard of in wartime.

By then he was going to work, and after Mother's death we lived altogether in one heap, and Sváťa was born, and I can't recall how we all managed to squeeze into that one-room flat. What did I know about my brother? Nothing apart from the fact he was always talking about his job. He would bring me home chemicals from the chemical factory where he worked and I would do experiments in the loft trying to make Bengal lights or turn water into blood — because I had to do everything I read about in books. But in fact the only thing I did with real enthusiasm was play soccer and mooch around with girls outside the Home for Mothers and Children.

My brother was too independent somehow, and when I was just starting to get my bearings he was already well established and making his way in the world. By general standards he was a successful young man. He had cars, for instance, when nobody else did. They were old bangers, but they were cars. He used to drive me to college in Brno in an old black Praga and we would hurtle downhill at almost 70 kph. I expect he loved those cars, but he was no car snob like many people are nowadays. They were his playthings. Eva, love, I'm sure you remember him driving us to Hukvaldy in his Škoda Rapid. The roof on that car could be let down, and you and Zdenka tied scarves round your heads and the wind whistled all around us. The sun shone, and I have never known such happiness since in an automobile. You were wearing a red-and-white dress, and everything was somehow so beautiful and jolly in an old-fashioned way, like in some short story by Hrabal.[36]

So I still don't know whether my brother had any agonizing moments of sorrow or doubt, whether he worried about things that were more than he could handle. He radiated an atmosphere of self-confidence and a belief that he was always capable of coping with everything and that nothing could put him off his stroke. And maybe he was just that sort of person. He was unusually self-assured in everyday matters. Probably only Zdenka knows about his doubts, his uncertainties, his sorrows, and

36. Bohumil Hrabal: 1914-1997, one of the best-known post-war Czech authors. His tragicomic fiction includes *Closely Watched Trains* and *I Served the King of England.*

his unrequited longings. I only ever saw him cry once, and that was when he returned breathless on his bike from Stará Ves to find Dad already dead. He grieved terribly then — he must have really loved Dad. During the next twenty years I only remember him laughing and beaming, calling me "bro" and hugging me — and he used to hug you warmly too, Eva. He knew how to radiate good cheer and warmth. Zdena would always be smiling happily at his side. He would often cuddle her in front of everyone and she would say: "Ouch, get off me!" (because he enjoyed displaying his strength). I always had the impression he had been happy for thirty years non-stop. Or maybe it was part of his character never to display distress. He never stayed in bed and never complained about anyone. And yet so many people burden us by griping about everything. He never did. He always treated other people with kindness and yet commanded their respect. Auntie Přendíková always used to say to me: "He's a good youth." It always struck me that he was spared all of life's minor tribulations, as if old lady Atropos knew she'd be cutting his thread earlier than is customary. Luck was with him: whenever we went picking mushrooms with him, the woods would be teeming; if I went alone I'd often come back empty-handed. He used to drive very fast but never had an accident. I don't recall his arousing anyone's envy. On the contrary, I had the feeling that no one begrudged him his success because he never flouted it. Even though he probably never read the philosophers and Kant would hardly have interested him, he carried within him, a priori, a moral foundation that enabled him to treat people right.

A pity I never saw him in the midst of that work that he passionately devoted himself to. He must have loved it because I never heard of him complaining about it. He was lucky in that respect, too. He seems to have enjoyed his work and been free of that common feeling of alienation. He did what he enjoyed doing and in addition managed to find plenty of other things that he enjoyed doing. I never saw him drunk. Only well-balanced people don't get drunk, even when they drink. Never in my life did I ever detect any dark corners in his soul. Though there must have been some, because we all have them. Maybe I suspected some of his frustrations and disappointments, but he hid them. He wanted to be a man and always stronger than me, whom he considered a kid in a carriage. He only displayed his feelings when he was cheerful. Mind you, I noticed that he was capable of gazing at Hanka with the helpless love of fathers who love their daughters too much. And I know he was deeply unhappy when he proved incapable of removing an obstacle from her path or when he couldn't cope.

Despite the fact that I regarded him with such affection, the two of us lived quite distinct and separate lives. I doubt that I was ever capable of explaining my world to him or what was important in it. He must have also realized that, although we were brothers, we were poles apart in our reflections on life and our way of thinking. He would always ask me over and over again what I actually did and was distinctly suspicious about the ambiguous status I enjoyed. It looked as if life held no mystery for him and that his practical designer's approach sufficed even for the gratuitous mysteries and esoteric problems that I dealt with. A pity we never found a moment to properly explain it all to each other. People like Fredo eschew warnings and are satisfied with the practical happiness represented by work and family, which are anyway the two things that make the world go round. Maybe it's just as well.

Not entirely, though. Fredo never managed to find detachment from his work. He allowed it to overwhelm him, not only with its rhythm, but also with the sham social significance that assumes the external form of office, authority, status in certain surroundings, etc. I still maintain that that was the greatest mistake he ever made. Because when later he was deprived of that sham status he was unable to come to terms with it, lacking any firm values to fall back on. All around me I would see people who suffered dearly for the loss of the sham social status that their work afforded them. They just couldn't renounce their attachment to it, and neither could Fredo.

3.29.1982

Over these past two years, I sensed the unhappiness he felt at being unable to continue the work he had committed himself to and how he fretted over the loss of social status and the cavalier way his talent and experience were treated, and all on account of politics that had never actually interested him and for which he obviously didn't have much understanding. It interested him only insofar as it affected his work, but he made no effort to identify the more complex factors that decide the fate of nations. Nevertheless, along with thousands of others, he paid dearly for having been in a particular place at a particular time and not on sick-leave or holiday, for instance, and having acted in accordance with the general mood and the most unsophisticated human attitudes. In that respect, during his last two years he actually fared worse than I, who was virtually forewarned and never taken by surprise. I was always intensively aware of the vicissitudes of life and always gave a bit of thought to how to deal with them. And always in terms of more permanent values than social status and the career ladder. But I didn't have the courage to impress on my older brother that he ought to drop everything, leave it behind him, and adopt a new lifestyle. I could see that he was too attached to his surroundings and was no longer capable of envisaging himself in a different way of life. I didn't even know how to explain it to him, or maybe it was because there were some things I hadn't yet experienced. Fredo simply couldn't draw a line under his previous existence and start afresh somewhere completely new. Even though he was best qualified to do so, and with his experience as a designer and his industriousness he could have made a go of it anywhere and wouldn't have had to wait on the clemency of those who don't know the meaning of the word. After all, he had the best possible support in his family and had no reason to fear poverty.

He must have lived in awful torment, otherwise there is no explaining his death. A heart attack is the slow sedimentation of inner anguish. Particularly when it assails a perfectly healthy person. Moreover, for years

Fredo had never had any opportunity to train for such distress. The neighbors say that on the morning of that fateful day he stood for a long time in the garden before leaving for work and gazed at that old pear tree in the middle of it. Maybe at that moment he had a vague premonition. Then he got into his car and drove off to his death. When one thinks of all the people who malinger — almost the entire nation, in fact — my brother never shirked his duties, neither on his last day nor at any other time in his life. It was something he ought to have done long before: to stop for a moment and take a look at the trajectory of human life from a greater height. Maybe he would have reached an understanding comprehensible to him alone, one that would transcend the everyday. It's something we all need in order to live.

It's possible that it wasn't like that at all and I am telling his story in terms of the coordinates of my own world, seeking for my own benefit an explanation for the absurd fact that Fredo would only be sixty years old and yet he is so many years dead. Maybe somewhere in the cosmos he was simply allotted that number of years, and the veins that led out of his heart were precisely programmed for that autumn day when I subsequently drove to Ostrava and reflected on the meaning of kinship ties. Ila and I were virtually left all alone and we Šimečkas started to disintegrate.

The reason I'm writing about it is to try to come to terms with it myself, in the same way that I'm having to come to terms with a lot of other things in my life. It's hard not to remember things here: memories arrive of their own accord and have an unusual intensity. After all, I'm always showering you with my memories, aren't I? I expect another reason I do it is that they make me feel good. Milan wrote at length about the urgency of reality. Sure, nothing beats submerging oneself in a reality ablaze with color and beauty. The trouble is that I'd sooner distance myself from reality, because it is repugnant and has nothing to recommend it. So I naturally turn to the intense reality of my memories and linger near them so as to know and understand them better. It takes two or three such inspections for me to detect what I often failed to see even when it was right in front of my eyes.

Well, on April 20 I expect they will all make their way to the cemetery at Zábřeh. Write and tell Zdenka, Hana, and Sváťa to take a few spring flowers from the garden and place them there as if I'd laid them there myself. And if you like you can send my recollections to Zdenka, though I know that her Fredo was someone else entirely. Throughout his life he was always more hers than mine, even though we came from the same nest.

Each of us has our own archive, Petr, and maybe you can imagine how much I'd give to be able to enter that time elevator of Asimov's and spend a short while in that old reality. Climb up on the handlebars of that magnificent green bike from Vybidlo with my brother in the saddle and go at such a lick that the palings to our right merge into a wall of light and shade. That would be something!

4.3.82
[Šimečka belatedly receives news of his daughter-in-law Marta's miscarriage]

I received another letter yesterday. The one from Milan. But it was sufficient. I scanned the first lines and it just made no sense. The shock emerged slowly from the letter, as if you'd deliberately engineered it to have the greatest effect. I read it right to the end and I seriously started to consider what I was going to do. And just as slowly it dawned on me that I couldn't do anything. All of a sudden I realized that I was getting worked up about an event that had occurred four weeks earlier. So I was a nonentity with no right to human involvement in life outside the walls of this cell, and there was nothing to do but to accept this reality and renounce any human reactions. The tragedy is that so far I have been unable to.

Because what could I do, in fact? Ponder on what it was like at Soňa's[37] when Marta went pale and nobody knew what the matter was? Ponder

37. Soňa Čechová: Marta's mother.

on what you felt, Milan, on that worst day of your life? And later when you discovered the origin of the threat to Marta? I did, of course. I cudgeled my brains, but with the feeling that I was solving a riddle that was solved long ago. That it was no longer a life-and-death riddle but simply a psychological quiz in some month-old magazine.

So to make things easier on myself I've opted for the only solution possible: today, Saturday, exactly four weeks after the operation, Marta is once more right as rain. She is even back at school and everything has ended happily. All the "what ifs" are over and done with. Quite simply, everything is sorted out. Nothing irrevocable has happened. This is the only way I can look at it, otherwise I'd probably find it hard to write my usual calm and detached thirty-page-long confession. So here is what I think:

You are all sitting together today in the quiet room on Vansova Street and no one is dwelling any longer on what might have happened. And in the garden Miluška's children are playing on the swing, like in the photograph I've got here. But I can't help sparing a thought for Soňa, who probably prayed — and prayed well — in spite of her atheism.

My thoughts are with Marta too, and suddenly I don't know what I'd say to her. Maybe only that she has unwittingly helped me to realize how supremely banal my imprisonment is. Things will turn out all right. But please don't any of you try to raise your spirits or relativize my fate in similar fashion!

I could naturally discuss with you at length, Milan, about the rights and wrongs and so on. You're right in saying that there is something primeval about the whole thing, and I'm almost ready to be believe that some Bad Fairy decreed that you should not be spared anything. Maybe she wants to test your soul. I expect you've been through something that is worse than anything I've experienced and you've faced up to things I've never had to. So in this case, it's me who'll be listening to you rather than trying to interpolate my philosophizing.

But it also strikes me that the trials we are facing should be enough for God. After all, haven't we shown proof of true Christian virtues, such as humility, love, and faith? So what more does He want? But, like you, I doubt the existence of some boundary beyond which mercy awaits us. Who knows? Maybe we've passed that boundary already. It would be nice to think so. If not, we'll have to make do with those three virtues.

By sheer coincidence I wrote in my last letter about how I selfishly expect nothing to change, how life will one day wash me up onto the shore at the point where I entered the water. Now I feel even more strongly what an illusion it is. And none of us can do anything about it. You ought to make every effort, though, to ensure that the changes which occur are part of a life of kindness that I could view with joy and not recall how many beautiful days were lost forever.

I expect in the coming weeks I'll be reading the sequel to this dramatic story and its happy conclusion. But so far I know so very little! From what Milan wrote, I deduce that you came back from the hospital in the middle of the story, Eva. And then you were at home with Milan. It must have been that way because I received the parcel of turnovers baked in our oven and then I got the apples and the cress, which I now have growing here. Let everything be the way I imagine it. Let everything be back in the old groove. Let the only new element be that in the hospital you made a fantastic recovery and your body chemistry sorted itself out. But next time spare me the beginning of dramatic events if I have to wait a week to hear the sequel. I have written to my counsel to call you and then send me a brief account of what happened. Such belated dramas as these are more than my nerves can take.

4.4.82

Now I don't know what to think. I just hope that I'll get something on Monday or Tuesday.

It's true they didn't renew my remand order as usual, but somebody was sent from the Prosecutor's Office to ask me whether I was satisfied with my accommodation. I told him I was and learned that the order was on its way and would last to May 30. So I'll celebrate the fateful anniversary here. I didn't expect anything else. I simply entertained a faint hope that I might be taking the bus to court and see Prague in the spring. But none of it is to be. But I did inquire of one of my fellow inmates who has already been to court what the spring looks like. He says the grass is sprouting green in the parks, they are selling flowers on the street corners, and he even saw some crocuses in magnificent bloom on a rockery in some garden.

The view from our window must be a joy to see now. I read in the paper that the temperature in Bratislava these days is 18°C., so I expect the forsythia is in bloom and the willow a fine yellowy-green. In the first letter I received while I was still in Bratislava you wrote to me how the spring was bursting out all around you. And now it will be doing it for the second time. I never knew how closely I was tied to nature. I tended to think of myself as someone with a restrained attachment to the beauties of nature. I was aware of them, of course, but I was too shy to be openly enthusiastic about them. In the mountains I would simply gaze in silence and the beauty would caress me pleasantly; only now do I realize that that silent adoration was profounder than the elated reactions I often hear. What I miss terribly are the ordinary natural occurrences. I try to read something from the sky, but there is so little of it, and anyway the distant view of a few apartment blocks is often obscured by smog over Prague. And it's an awfully long time since I last saw clouds that change color and are driven by the wind. I can't wait for my first storm.

So in fact, all I do is remember. But Milan is right when he says that you have to experience the reality of nature at first hand to be fully aware of it. People who come to me in my memories are alive, while nature recalled is dead somehow. If I were suddenly offered various earthly delights, I would spurn a prisoner's usual yearnings and invite you, Eva, to take an ordinary walk with me. I wouldn't need any broad vistas, magnificent peaks, or a sea of forests. Just take a close look at everything that is green, growing, and blooming.

Do we still have the plant guide at home? Why is it something we never paid attention to? All the things we missed. I never knelt down with book in hand to decipher the mystery of some plant: to ascertain the number of stamens, the shape of the stigma, and similar things I only remember from school. I never really believed you knew the names of those meadow flowers. Whenever you said something was goose grass or a pasqueflower, I always took it with a pinch of salt. All it needed was the will and I could have found out all sorts of things. Milan, take a lesson from my self-criticism and try to catch up if possible. After all, you don't even know that the white flowers you took to Marta at the hospital were narcissi — they couldn't have been anything else at this time of year.

I now have the feeling that it was a mistake to have stayed indoors when I could have gone out. But it wouldn't have been any good. It's impossible to acquire enough experience of nature to last forever. Such memory sources slowly dry up and leave empty-handed. But the people who set up the prisons definitely thought that what people miss most is being able to go out to the pub for a schnitzel and a beer. Not a bit of it — I'd opt for something quite different.

Only last year I read Theodore Dreiser's *The Financier*, or whatever it's called. After various unsuccessful speculations the hero ends up in prison. At the end of the last century. Although in solitary confinement, he has his own little garden where he grows flowers. Like in all books here, those parts were underlined and exclamation marks were drawn in the margins. This is how prisoners alert the reader to descriptions of prison life, and apparently they reach the conclusion that things used to be better than nowadays. Mind you, that doesn't apply to the description of the prison at Bologna that I found in a life of Michelangelo. But I noted with astonishment that Dostoyevsky in the *House of the Dead* had his own cook, and for a ruble he had a pound of beef a day. That I found incredible. It's interesting how I now remember the prison conditions of all the books I've read. I thought the most comical description was in Ivan Olbracht's[38] *Barred Mirror*. Sometimes I think of the conditions enjoyed in prison by the murderers and terrorists of the Baader-Meinhof

38. Ivan Olbracht: 1882–1952, Czech author and journalist.

group, how they were allowed radios and tape recorders and could have visits in their cells, because it is inhuman for a male prisoner to be separated from his wife or partner. A world of difference!

4.5.82

I had a visit from my advocate before lunch today. You had telephoned him, so he told me. It concerned the fact that some of us had been released from detention. Lady luck was in the vicinity but passed me by. But you didn't give him any news about yourselves or Marta. I just have to assume that everything is fine, otherwise I expect you'd have sent a message. You are always looking after me and forget that I'm looking after you. You must have suspected that I would be eager for news about you. Well, I'll make do with the thought that all the dramas are probably now all happily resolved, with the exception of mine.

Don't think I didn't care when I heard that some of us were already at home and sitting with their loved ones around the dinner table or warming themselves in the sunshine somewhere in the country. But for heaven's sake, what can I do but wish them all well from the bottom of my heart? I search for a shadow of envy within me but can't find one.

The news simply got me out of the depressing habit of not expecting anything good to happen. I imagine how it must have been for them when the cell door opened and they were told to pack their things. I didn't even hear lady luck as she passed by. She must have stolen past my door very quietly so that I wouldn't hear a thing. So I went on sleeping peacefully, and all I can think of now is how terribly disappointed you must have been, Eva my love. Maybe you were watching out for me again and I didn't even give a thought to it. Yet somewhere a decision was taken, a glimmer of hope flickered for a moment above us. It flickered and then went out.

Now I realize how little thought I give to the fact that all those hopes, and indeed the entire substance of our lives, is in human hands. Somehow I forget it and always end up thinking that my fate is somehow determined by an extra-human chain of contingencies and mysterious correlations. It certainly looks that way . . . Because when I consider it all in terms of human decision making, I fail to detect any human logic. So I prefer to stick with my old belief.

About a couple of weeks ago, Eva, I sent you a naive poem hidden in an acrostic. It was about us warming up in the April sun. And today I really did warm myself. We didn't get our exercise until the afternoon, and a band of sunlight shone into the exercise yard. I stood and faced it, letting it bathe my face and entire body. It was so splendid I almost wept with emotion. I must have forgotten because I was astounded by the enormous power of the April sun. It was scorching hot and blinded me even through my closed eyelids. When I opened them I could hardly see anything. The sky was pale blue and the sun was just an intense glow that I couldn't meet eye to eye. Soon I was marvelously warm and my prison sweatsuit was burning my thighs and chest. I prayed for it to last forever. I stood with my face to the sun and suddenly forgot where I was, overcome with the feeling of peace and happiness you get when lying on a beach. Everything was flowing out of me and all I could think of was the glowing star to which we owe our lives and which we treat in such paltry fashion. I realized the mental pressure that such a star can exert on people through its radiation, transforming them according to its moods. I submitted to it, trustingly surrendering to its power. It was a splendid moment and raised my spirits enormously. When I returned to the cell, I was blinking like a bat and it took me some time before I could sit down and write this. Maybe the sun will be shining tomorrow too. In fact, it ought to go on getting hotter, because it is outside human control and no one has the power to extinguish it, thank God for that. If people had the power, they'd have done so long ago to stop it shining into their neighbor's garden.

Take a leaf out of my book, Eva love. Take an armchair out to the balcony, shut your eyes, and think about nothing but that star that is constantly exploding somewhere in a nuclear conflagration. Don't even think about me, just about the star. You'll feel better for a while, you'll see, the way I did in that yard.

Petr, I learned from Milan's letter that you managed to go skiing again. I expect it's not enough, two weekends out of a whole winter, but it's not too bad when you think of all the winters you still have ahead of you. I also heard that you've lost your assistant and have to do everything yourself. So I picture you up to your eyeballs all day in dirty washing and other important things and console myself with the thought that in your case fleeting time holds out the promise of something better. Milan wrote something about 205 days, but it's already April 5, so I've worked out on a piece of paper that today you have precisely 179 days left, the number I reached ages ago when I was calculating my time in prison. That is before I gave up. I would so much like you to be back with Mother again. Milan has so much on his shoulders, and as you know he tackles every burden responsibly. He's incapable of tossing anything into the ditch. Instead he must transport everything to its destination, unload it, sort it, and thoroughly evaluate it — more than once, in fact, if it isn't completely clear to him. I hate to think how he must have tortured his brain trying to come to terms with Marta's illness. And you know everything about Mother. Everything has been in vain. She goes on telling me over and over again that she can't live without me. It gets me down. I don't know what compromise they reached. I don't even know what the trouble was. I think that I already wrote to them that they are the same old conflicts of judgment. You know as well as I do that they are trifling matters, but they represent conflicting attitudes to life. In Milan's reality all values are strictly classified, and he refuses to let lesser values interfere with higher ones, and sometimes they have to give way if for no other reason than to avoid confusion. It's a concept of reality that I fully share. None of us doubts that Mother's reality essentially shares the same hierarchy of life values. But in addition, she holds to some age-old belief that the fire must be kept burning at all costs. I mean this figuratively. It was the attitude of the matriarch of the species that the fire must be protected come what may. Even if half of the men failed to return from the mammoth hunt, the fire in the cave had be burning whatever happened. Our Mother doesn't guard any fire, because all you need to do is strike a match and you immediately have a blue gas flame. As you yourselves discovered long ago, instead of the fire Mother takes care of the day-to-day running of things and wants order in them. None of the three of us is fully capable of appreciating it, most likely because we have never known the desolation and depression engendered by a cold hearth, dirt, and disorder. I know it only from hearsay, and it must have been dreadful. Therein lies the origin of our conflicts. We are all focused on the clear centers of our realities, while Mother also wants the paths surrounding that center to be properly sprinkled with sand. What I'm saying is neither entirely simple nor largely symbolic. It's hard to explain, but I'm sure you grasp my meaning, including Mother. I can confide in the two of you that Mother has always reminded me of Susan in *Swallows and Amazons*.[39] Even if the boat capsized, the most important thing was to dry the crew's clothes so that no one caught cold. Even when the Swallows were about to embark on their greatest adventure, the first thing to be done was wash the frying pan and get Roger off to bed in time. This is something to which I have often given a lot of thought. Let us concede just slightly that the age-old habit of maintaining the normal cultural traits of the human species at all costs was somewhat more than a mere fetish of civilization. Maybe it is easier to face death when one has first brushed one's teeth. But that's not something I'll pass judgment on.

You see, boys, these things are no longer a mystery for me, and I don't even try to change anything. I'm sure you were also attracted by romantic Titty, who made spells with smelly wax to bring the Amazons luck. But maybe you'll eventually realize that it's much better to spend your life in Susan's tent. I don't want to oversimplify things in any way. I am sufficiently familiar with those two at home to know that I will not banish the differences between two concepts of the world by advising Milan to tidy up his running shoes, or not to spend more money than he has, or only to take the car when it's impossible to go on foot. It would be equally

39. *Swallows and Amazons:* The celebrated adventure story for children by the English author Arthur Ransome; the youthful protagonists, who spend their vacation sailing a dinghy in the Lake District, include the sisters Susan and Titty and their younger brother Roger.

unwise to advise Mother to stop washing the floor because I happen to have a toothache in my heart. It's all a matter of recognizing that our realities are never identical and not even their centers necessarily overlap. But we realize how important it is that they do overlap. As I said already, I have all the advantages. My realm is several meters square, and I don't have to take care of anything. Soon they'll bring me supper and it will be the usual Monday fare of sauerkraut, potatoes, and blood pudding. I don't have to pay for it. I get it free now. In fact, I'm a man with no problems.

4.16.82

Eva my love, all the time I've been here I've been trying to comfort you. In those first ten letters that you didn't receive I actually lectured you, arguing that you were and are capable of leading a meaningful life; it might not be a cheerful one, but you could at least manage a serene smile. However, to judge from your letters, my theoretical instruction doesn't seem to have had much success. We have a whole long year behind us and by now we both realize that theoretical assumptions and practice can diverge. It's harder than we were ever capable of imagining, isn't it?

And yet, in spite of everything, it has been a year that will most likely be of deeper significance for our relationship than the previous years altogether. We were both covered in a layer of dust left by the recent years of tiresome ordinariness. We tried to shake it off all right, but you know full well that it was not easy. All the wrongs done to us came in measured-out doses. We ended up spending more and more effort maintaining an acceptable face on our everyday existence in order to retain a bit of happiness within it. Even the happiness that life vouchsafed us was often difficult for us to see in proper proportion. It became obscured by cares and overburdened by the mere needs of working, earning a living, and ensuring at least minimal prospects for you and the children. We each endured it in a slightly different way, as you're aware yourself, aren't you? You lacked the ability to forget about it all and live for the few things left us, which many others might willingly take in exchange for all their prosperity and peace and work and prospects. That period went on for quite some time, heaping dust onto our relationship, too. It was a very fine dust, almost imperceptible, and it's even possible that we thought our faces were clean. But we both know that there were moments when we found the dust suffocating. You in particular had the feeling that there was nothing to enjoy any more, nothing to satisfy one's inner needs and hanker after. In all the discussions we had, no matter about what — new shoes for me, painting the apartment, the weekly budget — the dust would rise and obscure our view. And then it would fall back on our relationship, so that every now and then we would have to shake it off, realizing that it mustn't happen, that there was something much more valuable at stake than everything else.

I have thought about it all quite a bit. I have carefully considered whether it wasn't insensitivity and selfishness on my part, all that frenzied flapping of my hands to ward off the dust. But no, it wasn't. It's something I just can't help. Maybe it's an innate need to have clean air around me. It's not a matter of pride as you thought — conscious disdain for the humility and devotion of "ordinary life." After all, I am humble towards life too and accept everything it brings me with reverence and composure. It's something else. Simply, I was unable to come to terms with the dimension of life that circumstances had foisted on me. You must know that I actually tried to. And before I discovered this about myself, I used to thrash about trying to discover where the fault might lie. That was years ago, and I expect I hurt you quite a bit as well as I lashed out. I had an oversensitive reaction to that dust and started to squirm as soon as I felt it on me. But I couldn't stand it on you either, which is why you came in for plenty of knocks, too.

I fancy that it doesn't have much to do with my writing, which, by the looks of it, is the reason for our precarious situation. I just used what I had at hand to prevent the dust from settling. But if I hadn't learned to write, I would have found something else to use. The fact of the matter is, it's not our fault. And by now you know that as well as I do. From the very outset we only wanted to make something of our lives. We even wrote about it in our notebooks. Some might maintain that we've made a proper mess of them! One in prison and the other, ill and without a job, cowering in an apartment with a tomcat. We quietly respond: we're thinking about what we've made. Milan is sitting and thinking about it, and Petr is thinking about it on his night duty, and all those that share our fate are thinking about it, and the end result of all that thinking is that we know better. Maybe, just maybe, we all know now that it's hard to live with all that dust in your hair.

Our relationship, our love, is part of those lives. We are too attached to each other for our love to be seriously at risk, but at the same time there was nothing to protect it from falling dust. And the dust settled on it in those situations when the worry about trying to maintain a civilized standard became too much for you, despite the fact that we faced no real risk of destitution. Or when you would torment me with your lamentations about my recklessness, which wasn't recklessness. The dust was settling when you were resentful about my stubbornness, which wasn't stubbornness, and my pride which wasn't pride. I simply tried to brush the dust off me each time. Above all when you were resentful about my writing, which was in fact no more than that. But I really want you — and the boys — to know that I know, and always did know, that the fruitless onslaught on my writing and what happened to it was solely motivated by *your fear for me* and, therefore, by *your fear for our love.* Because you felt that without me there wasn't any love. You'd always emphasize magnificently that you're an ordinary woman and an ill one to boot. And to tell the truth I was pleased — and still am — that as an ordinary woman you love me. Perhaps Milan will find this hard to understand, but what is there to understand about a wife wanting above all else to have her husband with her? She just wants to live with him and is resentful, fearful, jealous, and frantic about anything that threatens the basic situation of their life as a couple, which is quite a different quality of life, as we know. Eva, love, I never underestimated your understanding for the wider implications or for the yearning for life's broader dimensions. Not even when you made a show of not giving a damn about any of it. It was enough for me whenever I was late coming home from work to read in your eyes the fear of an ordinary woman for her husband, the terror of being left alone and the collapse of everything. That fear was part of our life and for ten whole years it consumed you. I was aware of it but could do nothing to help you, because if I'd taken the opposite path we would have been at greater risk: slow suffocation under a layer of dust. Our love would have been the first to die. And that would be the worst thing that could befall us.

4.18.82

After all that has happened, things with us are like after being caught in a rainstorm in the woods. The first thing we notice is that our hands and faces are clean — all the dust is gone. Then we realize that a lot of other things have also disappeared, washed away, among them the ordinary joys of life that you took care of so passionately. Plenty has been washed away. A whole year has gone by without any intimate contact. You are being put to the test in a way you never dreamed could happen. But just look at what we have left. Our relationship is free of dust. Which of us recalls how so thick it was with dust we could hardly breathe? Not me. Do you? How many people can say the same? When I received your first wholehearted letters, full of the warmth that was shy to express itself in that dusty everyday existence, I strode around my cell with joy in my heart. I could share it with others. Though the equal of all the other unfortunates here I nonetheless felt myself the richer by several lives, and Petr and Milan's letters heightened the feeling. It wasn't sadness, but nostalgia. The greater the love, the greater the nostalgia. This direct ratio makes it terribly hard to bear, but believe me, I would sooner have this dreadful nostalgia than the sort of torpid depression caused by estrangement and desertion that I've seen plenty of here.

You write to me that you are incapable of taking it this way, that the longing is worse than all the rest. I don't entirely believe you. You don't long for any old me. You long for me the way I am. It's hard to say, but maybe I could have been back with you ages ago, but you might not have recognized me through the layer of dust. Even an ordinary wife can appreciate that, I should think. What would I mean for Petr and Milan at that moment? Is it my fault that I'm aware of all that and I'm more terrified of frustration than of this nostalgia for a full life? Don't tell me you don't understand that, my ordinary wife.

The direct ratio of love to longing is constant. I miss you so much because I love you so much, because there was that storm and here you were standing wet and wretched, with bedraggled hair and no lipstick, but without the dust of those mutilated years, like that time when we were caught in that storm on the way to Kraľova studna. It's like a law of nature: love always has to be redeemed somehow or it goes to seed. It's fine now that I can love you with your "I love you and will love you come what may." Because it is through adversity that we redeemed our love. The way I feel you next to me here today, your are a new Eva and also — just slightly — an old one — the Eva from the time of your first enthusiasm, full of courage and determination in the realization that love comes first and all the rest follows. A self-confident nursing mother in a room that wasn't much bigger than this cell. You are new for me in the sense that you have shed your doubts about which me you love. Or haven't you? Of course you have. I can see it in your eyes when we have that half-hour together. Don't worry, I'm perfectly sober. I know full well that you are also a tortured soul, despairing at the mess of this world and that you'd be ready to sacrifice a lot of things for a bit of happiness and the security you deserve. I know that you haven't had too much of the joys of life over these past years and you ask yourself, "Why should I live this way when others . . ." I know you're ill and at certain moments of chemical imbalance your mind flutters helplessly in the face of life's enormous demands. I know all that, and still I'm happy that I can love you in your old-new guise. And if you have enough imagination you know already what that means for me. I relish like a child every affectionate word you write me.

Maybe you'll say that everything I've said here is just abstraction, the output of a brain placed on a table like in one French sci-fi book. But my brain also knows that life has other delights apart from pure thought. After all, I've already written plenty about my natural yearnings and I tremble for the warmth of your nearness. But if I didn't strive to keep those ideas pure I'd probably die of emptiness. I relativize where I can, but there are truths that I have to hold onto, like the handrail in the tram, to stop being thrown from side to side. What I wrote you was one of those truths, and I believe it's one of yours, too.

I did get something yesterday after all: your letter and the card from Malino about the sun, the whiteness of the snow, the gullies, spring, beautiful days, twisted ankles, and how you are all thinking of me. I'm really very pleased that you could have that beautiful experience.

You wrote to me on March 24. At that time Milan also wrote to me about how they were expecting me. So now I know all the ins and outs. I could tell a sentimental tale that could have happened but didn't:

I really did arrive, and as Milan had planned, all of us, including Marta, went to visit Petr. He rushed out of the gatehouse and we hugged each other so hard we almost fell over. He regretted terribly that he couldn't join us. I'd have given all I owned if he could have come along, but he couldn't.

We reached Ružomberok[40] just in time to catch the last funicular. By now there was no snow at the bottom, but as I was carried higher and higher the woods started to turn white and pink in the setting sun. I was warm in my anorak and I just stood and gazed. My eyes devoured the trees, the distant mountains, and the chimneys of Ružomberok. Marta was watching me, so I gulped back the tears at that immense space that opened up before me. Milan said nothing, but his eyes told me how happy he was for me.

I was climbing up to meet you and my heart thumped in my chest. We asked at the hotel for directions to our chalet. It was only a short

40. Slovak town between the Great Tatra and Lower Tatra mountain ranges.

step but we walked slowly to make the moment last for ever. We saw smoke rising from the chimney and suddenly I was terribly afraid that I wouldn't survive that moment and would drop dead on the snow. All the adrenaline in my bloodstream thundered in my heart and brain. So I told the two of them to go and tell you to come out and I would stay where I was and gaze at the white hill because I was rooted to the spot.

So off they went, and I followed them with my eyes. Then you ran out, suspecting something, and from a distance I could see those wide eyes and the anxiety in them that I might be what you feared. And suddenly you caught sight of me standing rooted to the spot. You started to run faster than ever in your life, so that you lost one of your slippers, but you didn't care. And I started to run and we ran to meet each other like Petr and Milan when one was in nursery school and the other in the nursery. We collided with such force that it hurt. All you said was "Milan, Milan" and I comforted you, though there was no need any more. And so we silently gazed at the mountains. I can't remember what was going through my mind — nothing, I was just aware of the setting sun and your nearness. We would have frozen to death in that pure air but the others were calling us in. So I gave everyone a hug and then lay down on the hearth. The logs crackled. From the kitchen wafted the scent of the chicken Marta bought that day in Ružomberok. You all had the fond notion that I would tell you something. Not a bit of it. I just lay on the hearth and stared at the burning logs. I stretched out my hands to the heat, then my legs and my back so as to drive that prison chill from my body. I quietly thought to myself that this cell was still standing here. Karel opened a bottle of red wine and I let myself be persuaded into having a sip. Then, feeling out of sorts, I went outside again to reassure myself that I was surrounded by the wide-open space of the woods and mountains. I touched you again to make sure. I went around touching and feeling everything like a blind man just to reassure myself. What a great story! It was too beautiful to happen, so I had to make it up. It's none the worse for that, though! When did it happen? Where is that mountain with the snow and the setting sun? Where is that hearth?

Where are you, my dear ones? A story is a story. I'll send it on its way like a ping-pong ball and it will bounce around my cell. I'll finish the page and then do some exercise.

4.30.82

I finished writing the last letter in the hopes that I might receive something from you, but I'm already starting another one a few days later and still nothing. I don't expect any news, as it's only been a week since your visit, but even so your letters make the day a holiday, and one that's no less festive than tomorrow's.

Well, here we are. It's the beginning of May and a year will have gone by. I can't even remember what sort of spring it was a year ago. But I doubt that it would bear comparison with this year's. It's hardly spring, anyway. There's a cold draft from the window, and my arms and legs are permanently cold as ice. Back at the beginning of April I was already looking forward to warming up a bit. I don't suppose it's any better in Bratislava.

Even so, calendar May will burst forth tomorrow inexorably. However, my experience of last year has stripped it of all the poetical mystique traditionally associated with this month. I won't be taking a walk on Petřín,[41] and I doubt that I'll hear the jug-jug of the nightingale. Prison doesn't sanction love.

And yet love finds a way from time to time. One can witness absurd love affairs and crazy emotional displays that are probably impossible under normal circumstances. While I was still in Bratislava I used to hear all sorts of professions of love flying from one window to another across the prison yard. They were voices of vain longing. Sometimes that longing would find direct and brutal verbal expression. On other occasions it was poured into utterances that were a match for any movie dialogue. In Bratislava I briefly shared my cell with a fellow who was by any normal

41. The hill in Prague where lovers traditionally gather on May Day.

criteria a burglar, no doubt about it. Yet he related to me a love story that I would never have expected of him. It was a short story of love for his own wife, whom he had married when she was fifteen and with whom he had two children. They lived together until his arrest, and, as he told it, they had never had a single quarrel but enjoyed a harmonious and passionate union. It was odd to be sitting in a prison cell in the evening listening to a plain tale of faithful, lasting, and unblemished affection of the sort one no longer hears in far superior company. He would dreamily tell me how he would go to meet his wife from the afternoon shift at the factory every evening at ten and how he would rub her all over with camphorated oil when they got home because her back ached from the work. He told me how in the evening they would watch their sleeping children with tears running down their cheeks, and many other things that sounded as if they had been copied out of romantic stories from the last century. And I would wonder to myself whether it wasn't simply self-deception designed to console himself. But no, I would have seen through a lie of that kind. It was an unconscious copy of Bonnie and Clyde, except that the young burglar would go out alone at night on his housebreaking forays, while his wife stayed at home anxiously minding the children. The genuineness of his feelings was beyond any doubt. This was no prison lie. The young wife was in the same prison, and when the women were exercising in the yard and my companion caught site of his love for a moment he would blench and his eyes would redden. It occurred to me that at any moment he would tear out the bars or punch his way through the meter-thick walls. I've never seen such an animal-like longing to escape, to break out of the cage. It was a story that combined, like in the old ballads, a total disrespect for society's laws with tenderness and love for a woman. If someone invented it nobody would believe it. But I am convinced it was so. It looks as if that whole romance came to an end because the burglar could expect a sentence of at least eight years. When I asked him why it all happened, he just shrugged and said, "I don't know, stupidity I suppose." He was twenty-five, she was twenty-two.

I heard a lot of other "May-time" stories. Some were moving, others were superficial and pathetic. But in the main they were accounts of wasted opportunities, which reflected the teller's awareness of how his life had been squandered. But it all simply confirmed my perception that love and all its possible deformations are an enormous motivating force in human lives.

You'll no doubt think it absurd that someone could fall in love in prison, and yet I witnessed that, too. I observed romances germinate from shouted conversations through a window, or through a stinking latrine pipe, or by means of smuggled messages — all those resourceful forms of "illicit contact" as the official jargon described it. To the ears of men shut up in cells, the dulcet tones of women's voices sound like the call of the sirens, even though most of those voices belong to young women with dubious pasts. But that doesn't matter here. I experienced real suffering on the part of lovers who had never set eyes on each other and whispered to each other through barred windows like Pyramus and Thisbe. In fact it went so far that I was consulted about the possibility of marriage, of which I knew nothing, of course. Naturally there is an element of fun involved — a welcome opportunity to shorten the dragging hours. But another reason for these absurd romances is the emotional aridity of their past lives and the months in prison. What probably makes it most attractive is the Platonic nature of such relations, which are untrammeled by facial appearances or physical proportions, let alone the conflicts of everyday life. They are Platonic orgies in places where one would least expect them. And all this in an era of casual sex and the coarsening of human relationships!

Oh well, it's probably on account of the spring. Tomorrow is quite simply the First of May, so it can't be helped, even though outside the window the couple of flags that I can see are being given a good buffeting by the freezing wind. I suppose that's why I automatically got onto this topic at the beginning of this letter. What am I supposed to think about this May? About what was or might still be? For the time being I have to breathe on my frozen fingers to keep hold of the pen. I can't wait to get into bed.

5.1.82

The big day woke me up with the howl of wind in the bars and a gloom that has not lightened even now after lunch. It's a strange May Day. It's raining, and there are even occasional flakes of snow. I read in the papers that there are 170 cm. of snow at Luční Bouda. If this is the Good Lord's idea of depriving others of what I am unable to enjoy, I wish he'd stop overdoing it.

I thought that I might overhear the music from the loudspeakers like I used to back home, but in Ruzyně all is quiet and there is nothing at all to suggest the big celebration. Branches virtually bare sway on the trees. In spite of myself, my thoughts return to those May Days in the hot sunshine and warm air. The two of us in just our Socialist Youth shirts. Even in the evening it was as warm as in summer. Someone ought to draw up a precise chart of meteorological data, showing how it was then and now, so that I might find out whether I'm just talking nonsense like some old pensioner sucking on his pipe. But no one will shake my conviction that in those days girls attended May Day celebrations in short-sleeved dresses and no stockings. After all, there are photos to prove it. Such as the newspaper picture we have at home in which the present American citizens Iva and Miluška, as well as Staňa Břeňová, are no doubt shouting something about peace or "Long Live the Communist Party" or "Comrade Stalin."

Even before then I gave a lot of thought to the headiness of those collectivist May Day celebrations and the price it exacted. I recall how I always used to be of two minds about it all. I took part both willingly and unwillingly in the processions. I somehow always lacked that inner spontaneity — I wasn't able to express spontaneous enthusiasm, and when I wanted to shout some slogan I felt awkward and was afraid of looking like a drunk. I know I felt bad about it and was angry with myself, convinced that I was at fault. It definitely wasn't because I didn't agree with any of the slogans that we were supposed to shout. I'm sure that at the age of twenty I regarded Comrade Stalin as a wise leader and leading light of science. I know I would guiltily avoid carrying flags and banners. But I also know that I adored the afternoon and evening of May Day, when we'd wander around Brno with our *Kultbrigáda* and sit in a drove in front of the House of Art or in the parks and sing daft songs and hold hands. We both had blue shirts, and in a certain sense we were intoxicated by the celebration. It was an odd, cheap sort of alcohol. I suspect we didn't even have to eat anything. And there was no organization. Our crazy group of young men and women must have looked to anybody of discernment like a gang of dangerous fanatics, though I don't recall our being linked by any negative emotion. It was all about trust, love, friendship, solidarity, and a craving for happiness. And yet it was not a time of universal trust, love, or friendship. On the contrary: here in Ruzyně many innocent people awaited death. I'll never know what I'd have done if someone had given me a sensible explanation at that time.

Nevertheless, I wonder whether the experience of those days means we have to totally renounce collectivism and its orgiastic delights or whether collectivist intoxication can still play a positive role in human coexistence. The point is that I have no overall awareness of any bad aftertaste — apart from shame at the stupidity — from the intoxication of that time; it's an intellectual hangover, not an emotional one. I definitely regarded the group of people around me as a bulwark, even for our purely selfish romance that wasn't constrained at all by being constantly surrounded by onlookers. Instead, I had the feeling that it was worth more on account of being looked at by others and that the onlookers were happy for us like an audience at a good play. Whenever I saw a couple huddled together in a park, I would be sorry for them that they were all on their own and had no one to share their happiness with. I had the feeling that a lot of people would like to join in our silly games, that they envied us our inebriation, and that only shyness prevented them from linking hands with us. It never occurred to me that the obstacle might be common sense, or some other experience of life that led them to regard the blue of our shirts as a hostile color. The tragedy of the whole thing was that such experience existed and we didn't realize it.

Nor do I think that the collectivist intoxication was the result of "ideological unity," or any of the idiotic guises that collectivism assumed at the time. Probably the deepest and most intoxicating experience of collectivism — I expect you'll agree — was the informal hillbilly-like existence of the work camp at the Kružberk Dam project. By then there were no formalities, and I cherish the memory of life in that old inn above the rising dam-lake as something exhilarating. I still feel a certain nostalgia for the security of a human group in which there was no time for even a speck of boredom and which was capable, quite democratically, of devising a life that was one joy and discovery after another.

Maybe that's why I am incapable of rejecting that sort of collectivism and giving pure individualism priority in all things. An affinity for the group is probably deeply-rooted in human beings (Mary McCarthy), and submitting to that instinct is rewarded by delights similar to when satisfying any other human drive. As in all other cases, failure to gratify natural instincts undoubtedly deforms human existence, probably in the same way as the denial of sex or motherhood.

But the whole problem is that collectivist intoxication is easily abused, as numerous instances in history testify. Moreover, like every instinctual intoxication, it eliminates reason's power of control. We ourselves were undoubtedly victims of such abuse for a time, although I'm not convinced that the abuse was deliberate and coldly calculated. The brains that controlled the forms of that collectivism weren't capable of such diabolical sophistication. Abuse like that occurs of its own accord and is virtually an automatic process. Even Savanarola was not such a cunning devil.

5.2.82

Those intoxicating May Days and all that youthful collectivism have now disappeared from the scene. They were part of a very particular epoch, and no one will revive them again. I expect that these days they would simply arouse astonishment and be a blatant anachronism. Nonetheless, it is quite likely that a longing for some collectivist intoxication of that kind slumbers in every human being and in the young most of all. Nothing like that can ever be organized again; people have to create their own sensible collectivism. These days, however, the civilizational framework is hostile to such collectivism. Free time is individualized by such technological apparatus as television, hi-fi, cars, bikes, etc. And when some of the boys here described to me in detail what it's like at the Prague discotheques or their various parties, I thanked my lucky stars that I'm not young at this time.

However, the hostility of our lifestyle towards collectivism will probably raise the value of the thrill it can offer. Let no one tell me that those semi-legal parties in the woods, if not parties in general, not to mention the free associations of beer drinkers that I've heard about here, as well as the many other youth groups that come into existence outside the official state-run organizations, aren't an expression of a natural group instinct. I have deliberately informed myself about them and discovered that those often strange and immoral groupings have many features in common with what once united us, above all an effort to escape isolation and a striving for understanding. I shouldn't think young people have ever felt as strongly as nowadays that all adults are a pack of idiots. I expect we didn't feel it to that extent, but after all we must have felt that way a bit, if only because the majority of adults did not share our naive belief in the future. These days belief is neither here nor there. What adults don't want to share with the younger generation is its frivolity and lack of respect for accumulated property. But that also doesn't apply without exception.

I can recall how when all that ceased to exist in our lives, i.e., immediately after we left university, I felt a vacuum, and when at the very beginning of my career I was left to my own devices in some kind of monastic boarding school, I felt as miserable as an abandoned puppy. There were plenty of periods like that, and all the groups that I joined subsequently lacked that original sense of intoxication. It was as if they were all undermined by competition for higher pay and bigger country cottages. In fact it wasn't until my downfall that I once more had a sense of renewed collectivism on a small scale in the circle of friends who had suffered a similar fate and were also seeking to reassess their seemingly wrecked lives. How wretched it would have been if I'd never rediscovered it. Naturally, latter-day friendships can't go in for the silly things we did in the fifties, but whenever we were at Hradeček,[42] for instance, or at our many evenings at the Kusýs' and elsewhere, I was able to revive my crazy forgotten attachment to the collectivism of my younger days, as I listened to the conversation, interesting tales, and ordinary silence. These days everything has a different name, but deep down it comes to the same thing. Among other things, it is a school for life situations, a harmless remedy for depression and constant experiments in transcendental being, because it is a way of breaking the bounds of one's own existence and finding others (Sartre).

Simply stated, there is something to it, and extreme individualism is often a virtue of necessity. It masks a failure to achieve that transcendence, or it masks a sense of personal worthlessness and a burdensome void in which there is nothing to offer. God forbid that I should advocate a new collectivism; all I'm saying is that natural instincts will always find a way to assert themselves, and whoever is reluctant no matter what to submit to them is slightly ill.

I don't know what experience you boys have in this respect or what judgments you have come to. Milan has experienced rather more than you, Petr, even though he has seemingly had less opportunity. What is astonishing is how the collectivist spirit has totally vanished from higher education where it is in fact most naturally at home. I don't know whether at least some slight sense of it can be felt in the army. Milan's letter from the Tatras contained an echo of that old intoxication when he wrote how he could hear in his and Marta's cabin the voices of their friends and how he felt his security and happiness was linked with a common snowy existence and the promise of an evening with pleasant, quiet chat.

42. Hradeček: the site of Václav Havel's country cottage, a haven for regime opponents.

When one realizes all this, it is necessary to make an effort. I'd say it was worth it. And maybe a new collectivism is coming into being after all, with a qualitatively different character than our old, voluble sort. Quieter and more inward looking. One that is self-sufficient and whose by-product might be creative activity, or at least some attempt at a life of dignity, one using such things as cutting wood, sport, literature, or good food as possible tools. Nothing is ruled out, as it's all human. I ought to write a few how-to manuals. I'd have the time, and I've got all sorts of ideas. The trouble is I feel I'm wasting space that should be used for conversation. It all got mixed into my letter on account of that cold May Day, and in fact last night the doors actually rattled in the gale, so we were obliged to stuff paper under them. So forgive me. I'm bound to receive something from you tomorrow and will be able to give you my full attention.

5.3.82

Still no sign of any post. But I've just bid farewell to my cellmate who spent the past four months and more with me. All of a sudden he's gone, bound for some prison camp, and I feel rather sad about it. He was the best companion I've had here in the entire year. He was extremely pleasant and friendly and almost an ideal type for this sort of coexistence. And it's a very specific sort of coexistence, in which one is constantly bumping into the other person. This man never failed to say sorry, so it was like being at some first night at the theatre, with sorries, excuse me's, and would you be so kind. It's naive, of course, but it's nonetheless a way of preserving a bit of human dignity.

We'd also play a lot of games together to help pass the time. I taught him German and he was the best pupil I've ever had. He would study diligently three hours a day and during the four months we managed to complete the teach-yourself textbook. He learned the entire vocabulary and a bit extra, as well as all the basic grammar, including the subjunctive, the conditional, and other brainteasers. Towards the end he was capable of conversing with me each evening slowly and carefully about everything imaginable, and he could actually write a letter or short composition almost without mistakes — the verbs were always at the end of the clause and the nouns were in the appropriate case after the prepositions. It could be that he learned more German than the great majority of high-school graduates. Achievements like these are indeed only possible in prison.

He paid me back by initiating me into the theoretical problems of electronics and electrical engineering, and in addition created dozens of acrostics and rebuses that are more difficult to compile than to solve. He was a self-made poet, and I carried out extensive textual analyses of his verses. Some of them were quite charming.

Now he's gone and I'll have to get used to other people and resist all the dangers of the submarine effect. I already feel like a permanent resident with successive lodgers. Goodness knows if I'll ever see any of them again. You live with someone cheek by jowl, and then all of a sudden they disappear from your life and you never see them again. But apparently that is typical of prison life. So the old-timers tell me.

courtesy of the Milan Šimečka Foundation

Šimečka shortly after his release from prison, 1982.

courtesy of the Milan Šimečka Foundation

with his son Milan (Martin).

When I started to write these long, separate letters about the nature of reality, I scarcely entertained the possibility that I might eventually send them or hand them to someone personally. In prison I consistently held to Dante's line and abandoned all hope lest I should suffer too much over their demise.

And lo, a year later, I'm sitting at home at my desk and reading what I actually wrote then and wondering why I wrote it and what to do with it. There is an enormous difference between the two situations: the one in which I wrote it and the one in which I'm reading it, and that difference perturbs me. I ask myself why I started to engage in philosophical speculations in prison. I was probably tempted by the scope it offered: I had a pen, paper, a table, and a gray wall in front of me. I didn't have bookshelves at my back to unsettle me — as they are now doing — coaxing me to correct the obvious lapses of memory and in general to somehow improve the carefree flow of ideas that I set down on copy paper in my cell. It also occurs to me that I should put the whole lot into a shoe box and leave it like that.

But at the same time I tell myself it wouldn't be fair. Now I've written something, you ought to read it. So I've copied out my discourse just as it was. There I didn't need to play the scholar, and it was marvellous to clamber up to the higher spheres of abstract speculation without fear of falling, except onto the hard stool — which I happened to be sitting on anyway.

I came to the realization that in certain situations playing with ideas is as fascinating as playing with a Rubik's Cube. If there's anything here you choose to give any credence to, fine, if not, that's all right, too. I say so in the light of the tolerance towards human reality that I advocate in all sincerity and that I regard as the best possible road to freedom.

Bratislava, August 1982

Dear Petr and Milan,

I read the letters you send to me here in prison over and over again and I discover that your thoughts often touch on questions which would certainly be nice to discuss somewhere sitting by a fireplace with crackling logs, or staring at a fishing bobber, or while walking in the countryside, as we often used to do. But since we've lost those opportunities, I'll at least try to imagine such a setting and quietly tell you what I think about it all. At the same time, I'll make the sinful observation that the actual surroundings in which I'm attempting this discourse is maybe more inspirational than that quiet spot by the river, where one is all too aware of nature's superiority, and its beauty and permanence definitely tend to slow the pace of one's thinking.

I'm not sure whether it's unusual, or on the contrary, quite natural that in this situation, in which all we can do is write to each other, you dwell more than at other times on age-old questions to do with the nature of reality and our ability, or lack of it, to perceive this reality in its true form. At the same time you raise the old desperate question about the truth of human perception in general, about people's various possible attitudes to reality, about the place of humanity in nature, and about the limits to human thought and action. And then, although you are reluctant to use the term, you raise the question of God, or in other words, of some order introduced into the world since its beginning that exists independently of mankind and is superior to it.

That's a lot of questions. We'd only need to add a couple more and we'd have all the questions addressed by the ancient philosophies. It's good that these questions present themselves to you in their original, ancient form, as they did in the days when philosophy wasn't yet ashamed of simplicity or coherence, or even of asking slightly naive questions. As you're aware, such simplicity is not encountered in modern philosophy, where a question posed in simple terms arouses amazement and sometimes even umbrage. And yet, as you know anyway, we have no more convincing answers to such simple questions than the old Platonists had, for instance.

I have never concealed from you that I have always treated all those things with enormous tolerance, that I've taken them as a kind of game and never entertained any illusion that the solution to those questions — the cracking of the nuts that people have broken their teeth on since time immemorial — would in one stroke solve all the ills of humankind and transform the human lot. The absolute majority of human beings are indifferent to such questions. Perhaps many of them realize that such questions exist and are aware of them through religious interpretations or occasional cozy debates. But most people are unconcerned by these issues and maybe only occasionally do they cause them a slight pang in some dim corner of their consciousness, like an old toothache. From your own observation of the world you are aware that most people have gotten used to the fact that one can get by in this life without philosophical conundrums, and it's even possible to lead a contented and cheerful life without any clear idea of the nature of the world we live in. In all events you've read about that sort of "being" in Camus and Sartre. The knowledge of our ignorance about the fundamental nature of things is not a condition of being. By now I am chary of asserting that thinking is a condition of being; I'm not sure that it is necessary to reflect incessantly on one's own life and cogitate about it. Maybe it meant something else when *cogito ergo sum* was all the rage. But I also think that one needn't regret the passing of utopian hopes that in the future all people would indulge in philosophy or even poetry. In fact, it's all to the good, because so far every attempt to make philosophy the property of all mankind has resulted in its degradation. In such cases, philosophy was always reduced to a few maxims and slogans, as happened to Christianity and Islam and is happening to newer doctrines, too. I can still well remember the period when philosophy was entirely derived from a slim booklet that was part of the Short Course of the History of the All-Union Communist Party (Bolsheviks) by J.V. Stalin. Such reduction of philosophy could indeed become the property of all mankind, but it would no longer be philosophy, just the parroting of a few philosophically sounding phrases. Philosophy must be voluntary and spontaneous — like any mental activity, in fact — or it's worthless.

Well in that sense the two of you are volunteers. No one forced you to read Russell, Sartre, Kafka, Camus, Bergson, Kant, Hegel, or all the other things you tackle. Even I didn't push you. As far as I recall I only ever bought you one book of philosophy: Marcus Aurelius' *Confessions*. And I did so with a conviction that I would never admit to publicly, namely, that everything one needs to know about philosophy is contained in ten or twenty of the best books, among which I include that Marcus Aurelius. All the rest we read simply to be well read.

But since you yourselves have felt the need to raise these age-old questions, to ponder their weight and analyze their aroma, which saturates human life, I won't deter you from it — particularly since, at the very outset, you sense that in the end you have to answer many of the questions for yourselves, as no philosophy on earth will provide final answers. It's an enormous advantage to realize it, or at least to have an inkling at the outset. I have to admit that I was always taken aback when I encountered people who treated these age-old questions with a kind of haughtiness that led one to believe that all the answers had been provided and everything was quite clear. Happily, there aren't too many people like that around, and apart from our state Marxism, I don't think there ever existed any widespread teaching that maintained it had answers to everything. Mind you, as I write this, I immediately think of Khomeini and several other phenomena of our crazy world, echoes of which reach me here, and I'm not so certain about my last statement.

Whenever we raise these age-old questions and try to answer them in all innocence and virginal ignorance, we end up looking like second-rate imitators, because when we then turn to some ancient Greek for help, we soon discover that he betrays a similar innocence to our own and would have given the selfsame answer. Again I'll say something that is strictly between ourselves: my underlying conviction is that philosophers over the past two and a half millennia have differed from one another only in style and terminology. The modern ones have an unmerited advantage, as they stand on an ever-growing mound of knowledge and command a better view of the surrounding terrain. The ancient Greeks had an enormous handicap when it came to the elementary laws of nature. We have at our disposal the fantastic resources of physics, chemistry, astronomy, genetics, cybernetics, and goodness knows what else. Even so, when you read some idea put forward by a modern author, you can't help thinking that you are only reading a variation on something said by some Greek philosopher that you vaguely remember from Diogenes Laertes. If you ever had the opportunity to read Plato in its entirety, you'd discover it comprised almost the whole of philosophy. And in your Marcus Aurelius you have ethics as a whole, freely available to emperor and prisoner, soldier and centurion alike. In the Middle Ages it was really no great misfortune if people studied only Aristotle. But they shouldn't have forced him down Galileo's throat. There would be no misfortune in some people reading only the Bible, so long as they didn't prevent others reading Darwin. It would be nothing particularly wrong in state-employed philosophers reading only Marx (except they don't); what is wrong is that they prevent others from reading something else.

I would simply add that it never upset me to discover that I was probably more stupid than an educated Greek Sophist who had never flown in an airplane and wouldn't know what to do with a pocket calculator. On the contrary, it's rather nice to realize that one's affinity with other people is not governed by how distant they are from us in time, but by their attitude of mind. Why should it bother me to feel a greater rapport with an 11th-century Franciscan monk I've just been reading about than with the prison warder walking up and down the corridor outside. That kind of affinity spans entire epochs, and we are much the richer for it. I'm not at all surprised that Petr finds more in common with a Roman emperor than with the First Lieutenant in his unit. It only goes to show that time is not such a destructive weapon of nature against human beings after all.

I never much liked books that treated the thinking of earlier ages as old junk. Books like that appear mostly during revolutions. A lot of people used to pay homage to Mayakovsky, for instance, but I don't remember anyone loving him. As you know, I've read almost every utopia I ever managed to lay my hands on. And what annoyed me about all those utopians was their megalomania, the bombastic assertion that so far humankind has been groping in the dark and only now does the age of enlightenment begin. The error of that has been demonstrated time and again. And yet it never stops being repeated. It must be part of human nature that we regard ourselves as cleverer than those who went before us.

In this opening letter what I've actually been trying to tell you by means of cautious examples is that over the last two and half thousand years no discovery has been made to rival in importance the invention of the steam engine or the transistor. But maybe I've also told you that I don't regard it as a reason for us to feel inferior. A question about the origins and nature of the world is of a different order than one about the causes of infectious diseases. The second sort is asked with the awareness that we are capable of finding a precise answer. The first kind of question is asked involuntarily, as a way of asserting our humanity. We ask it even though we know in advance that the answer we receive will be only one of many and that there exists no arbiter anywhere in the world capable of confirming the correctness of any particular answer.

Well, finally, I have to warn you about believing these prison speculations of mine. You know yourselves that I've never particularly engaged in this sort of philosophizing. I was always more attracted to concrete social observation than to speculative fun. I expect it wasn't in my nature. It has taken this era of banishment and enforced contemplation to drag my spirit across the metaphysical threshold.

1.

When I assemble all the questions you've raised and referred to in your letters, they all seem to point to one central question, namely, *the nature of reality*. (In fact it's the reality that Milan experienced so intensely that time in the snow-covered valleys of the Tatra Mountains.) So I join you in asking whether there exists just one single reality, independent of human beings, which can be perceived from outside and described statically. But this also automatically begs the question how we as people relate to that reality and how it relates to us. I could also ask who established this reality and who gave it the laws by which it operates. One could also ask about the origins of language that articulates those laws, and we could go on asking more and more questions until we soon had a headache. You are bound to sense how asking questions in this way breaches the dike holding in all the speculative philosophy accumulated over the millennia. And it's not easy to keep oneself from drowning in the flood. One simply has to learn to ignore the flood as a whole and just concentrate on one coherent trickle. Otherwise one would have to abandon all such speculation at the very outset.

I first started to speculate on all this on a fairly modest scale and even out of a kind of practical need. It was during the first two months, at the time of the interrogations. Almost every day I had to answer a whole series of mostly senseless questions, and I suddenly became aware of a disturbing phenomenon: it was a constant vague feeling that those questions were drawing me into another reality that was not identical with my own, and which was possibly even different from the reality I had previously considered universal. I had the impression of being forcibly transferred to a reality that was specially manufactured and modified to make one lose one's way in it, lose contact with one's own reality, and eventually lose one's wits. Of course I realized right away that I was familiar with it from literature, that it was all to be found in Kafka, but now I was capable of fully experiencing Kafka for myself. Previously I had only read him.

I can't recall ever previously having such a powerful sense of differing realities or such a clear awareness of my own reality. That awareness of two realities started to fascinate me. I would look for the symptoms of such disparities until it almost became an obsession and I almost became indifferent to the other aspects of my situation. Eventually it proved quite a pleasant distraction, as it pushed gloomy thoughts about my future to the back of my mind. By chance I happened to have received a copy of Asimov's sci-fi novel *The End of Eternity* from the prison library. At one time we had a copy of it at home and both of you read it. Only this time I read it differently. It wasn't too hard to disregard the time leaps and ponder instead on the term "change of reality." I asked myself why such a change of reality didn't seem particularly absurd to me all of a sudden. I suddenly realized that in the course of those interrogations I was experiencing just such a change of reality. I sensed quite clearly that another reality was being foisted on me in place of my own, one that was altered for the purposes of the police. I couldn't help noticing that the two realities confronted each other and they were mutually unintelligible and incompatible.

At first it occurred to me that it was perhaps due to a difference of terminology, that the two realities — mine and that of the police — differed from each other because they each used different words and the phenomena of the two realities were called by different names. So I started to insist that terms from my own reality be used in the statements, such as "book," "essay," "study," "article," and "letter" in place of the police term "writing." I objected, for instance, to the use of the police phrase "made contact with" in statements, and in such contexts would dictate expressions from my own reality, such as "I made the acquaintance of," "became friends with," "paid a visit to," and so on. At that moment it seemed so important to me that I wrote a complaint to the Prosecutor General's Office even though it was undoubtedly a ludicrous thing to do. Nonetheless, the complaint was successful and from then on I wasn't prevented from using language from my own reality in the statements. Only I quickly discovered that in fact nothing had changed, that it had done nothing to end the mutual unintelligibility of both realities, and they still remained inert and hostile to each other.

It was only then that slowly, and almost against my own conviction, I started to admit the possibility that there could exist two different realities, mine and another that was the reality of "the investigating operatives." Thus in a roundabout way, and actually out of practical necessity, I started to contemplate the world as a set of realities of different kinds and to abandon my old concept of reality as the shared property of humanity as a whole, a kind of shared house that we all inhabit and are familiar with and that has stood here for us since time immemorial. In fact, we all view reality in this way. There are moments, however, when we have a sense of total helplessness, when we realize how differently just two individuals are capable of perceiving one and the same thing, and when moreover we ask who actually built the house for us and why, and what the expression "time immemorial" even means.

In my specific case it wasn't too hard to discover why my reality and the interrogator's reality differed. They differed from each other in precisely the same way that the two of us differed. The ludicrous terminological dispute arose because in my reality any written text expressing the ideas of human beings has the nature of a cultural artifact and becomes something inalienable. Indeed, in the case of an entire book, it becomes something almost devotional, since it embodies people's thinking and ideas, which are themselves an attribute of humans as a species. In my interrogator's reality that selfsame book, those selfsame ideas, were mere dross, something redundant and even harmful. Essentially they were just words written down, whose value was no different from the value of the words printed on a tram ticket. The difference between our realities was not only the result of our different attitudes to free and independent ideas, it was also determined by our different life stories.

It's true that I too expressed the doubt which you also might voice, namely, whether that difference might not simply be the result of a different attitude to the same phenomenon of a common reality, and whether the difference might not be explained as an expression of different opinions. But I suddenly felt that this was an inadequate explanation, that we didn't simply differ in our opinions about the same thing, we actually found ourselves in the middle of two different realities that met only at their borders. As I pursued this idea, I totally ruled out the possibility that it might be simply a matter of a different attitude and terminology. I suddenly saw that the "polymer" concept of reality fundamentally altered my attitude to a whole number of axioms of my thinking that I had previously taken for granted.

My reality not only differed from my interrogator's, it was also more spacious in a sense. My interrogator's reality was contained in my reality and was cognizable within it: I was able to analyze and understand it. But at the same time, I sensed that my reality was not cognizable within the interrogator's reality. Quite simply, it lay somewhere beyond the frontiers of his world, in a no man's land marked *hic sunt leones*. This greatly disheartened me, and I came to the conclusion that neither I nor he were at fault – the difference between our realities was due to the difference between our lives.

I will give another banal example in support of this gloomy conclusion. On many occasions I was asked the question why I had "made contact" with some person or other or why someone else had "made contact" with me. I would reply that I had made contact with the person in question because we regarded each other as interesting human beings and had the feeling that we might become friends. That plain affirmation, which was part and parcel of my reality, simply did not exist in his. He was therefore convinced that I was prevaricating or trying to be funny. In my interrogator's reality there existed solely utilitarian relationships between people. In his reality, the situation had never arisen in which someone would pay him a visit solely to make his acquaintance, and he had never heard of anything of the kind. In his reality, human relations were governed by practical considerations and simple objectives. One person went to see another only when they needed something from them, such as a cigarette, money, or sexual gratification.

These are banalities, of course, and I only refer to them so that you might get some idea of my despair and the sense of futility I felt as I observed the incompatibility of our two realities. But it was an exceptional situation, or a "limit situation" as the existentialists call it. But I can recall, and I expect you can too, countless occasions in totally ordinary situations when I've experienced this depressing disintegration of reality that we sometimes ascribe to our inability to expound our ideas convincingly. Alternatively, we get annoyed with others for their inability to understand us, or we simply take all these feelings of despair and without thinking twice toss them onto that enormous heap of sadness that has been termed in our epoch the impossibility of communication. Without wishing to apply this notion of "polymer reality" extensively, I would at least suggest that the main cause of all misunderstandings among people are individuals' differing realities. How many times in our lives do we find ourselves in a position of total helplessness in the face of a complete lack of rapport, and all our attempts at mutual understanding come to grief. As hard as we try, nothing helps. Such cases cannot be explained in terms of ill-will or the inadequacy of speech. It is quite simply a futile attempt to reconcile two realities which are naturally incompatible. As we know from chemistry, substances combine to form compounds only if they have the necessary prerequisites. And I would immediately add that the possibility or impossibility of joining two realities is the source of the tragic tension of human life, all that tension which tries to surmount the "non-conducting" insulation between human beings, everything that assists the spark to jump from one human being to another. So here you have it all: an explanation why on the one hand there is love, friendship and profound understanding, resulting from the favorable valences of reality, while on the other there is loneliness, rejection, and despair, all of which result from the "incompatibility" of individual realities.

2.

You can see for yourselves, my dear boys, how well everything fits together. Only I expect you can sense that it is hard to pursue these ideas for long in a state of philosophical innocence. We sense that this concept of reality, which assigns a different reality to every individual, inevitably moves us in the direction of Bishop Berkeley's teachings and that destructive solipsism that our mutual friend Winston Smith fought so furiously against in a situation similar to my own. But I tell myself that things needn't yet turn out disastrously.

After all, I haven't said that no other reality exists but the one appertaining to each human being. I don't deny the existence of a world in which everything we know and don't know happens. Nor do I deny the "existence" that is to be found only in books of philosophy. On the contrary, I feel an enormous humility towards the world and that reality which manifests itself as a combination of chemical elements, space, time, and electromagnetic fields — the reality that predated the human race and will most likely outlive it. Everything I say is out of deference for the depths of the universe, which I have not explored, of course, but which nonetheless exerts an enormous psychological pressure on me when I look up into the night sky. Both of you are aware of that and have written to me about it. I feel the very same pressure when I observe how the cress seeds start to sprout when I pour a drop of water onto the cotton wool. Nature and the world around us exert that pressure from morning to night. It is not simply a pressure but also a consolation — as you well know — because it confronts human stupidity, cowardice, and aggression with the peace of the universe, the stability of the mountains, the constancy of the tides, and so on. I sincerely admit that all of that is the main justification for the assertion that one cannot deny the world, and all other arguments I happily leave to the tender mercies of debate. As you know from the history of philosophy, not all the arguments advanced against that assertion have been entirely stupid.

Furthermore — and I'll say it straight away to avoid talking at odds — I believe that the world we live in is material, i.e., in the sense of the old philosophers, not in the sense of the "objective reality" that Soviet philosophy excised from Marxism. However, even this assertion is the product of psychological pressure. That pressure is exerted by our entire experience, both mental and practical. This affinity for the materialist approach to the world is bound to be the outcome of natural knowledge as well as of the anti-natural activity that materializes, for instance, in the combustion engine or the atom bomb, which operate so effectively. But as you see, I say this with a certain flippancy, because I don't believe that precise knowledge about the essence of the universe is of such decisive importance for humankind. It makes no difference to one's place in the world if one believes in the unending cycle of matter or in the spiritual origins of the entire universe. Neither belief helps to clarify the nature of reality.

I can assure you that I have never debated these things with anyone, but on the contrary have enjoyed listening to others expound on them with style and enthusiasm. And there was a time when I even had to conceal my liking for Plato's elegant speculations on the existence of a realm of pure ideas as a prefiguration of our own world. I enjoyed it as an enormous poetical concept that also exerted a certain psychological pressure on me. Who has never felt like an inhabitant of the cave in his attempt to penetrate the mysteries of reality? Plato takes away the anxiety we feel as cave dwellers by his soothing assurance that everything is beautiful, that the clear sun of truth is shining outside and all we need to do is head in its direction. After all, we have some inkling of the sort of pressure the idea of God exerts on people, because it takes away the burden of doubt. God comprises all mystery and uncertainty and ideally overcomes all contradictions. He removes the absurd surface from many things. He helps one understand time, as He has always been here and always will be. He created everything, and why that way and not any other is not our concern. Well, and why shouldn't God take a fancy to create the world using that particular combination of chemical elements that we are familiar with from Mendeleyev's tables? God is bound to have believed most of all in the possibilities of matter, since he created it. If it wasn't worth anything, He wouldn't have created it.

I'm convinced that people almost always formed their beliefs and notions under some such form of psychological pressure. And for that reason, monist ideas are of equal worth. It is one and the same concept of reality. From that point of view, one may now only regret all the energy that was wasted in the disputes among the major monist interpretations of the world. Materialism and idealism always tried to drag their opponent onto the playing field where the home team had the advantage. Purely in terms of philosophy, leaving aside ideological considerations, it is even impossible to explain why the quarrel was so acrimonious. The dispute between the nominalists and the realists had an inner logic at least, whereas the quarrels between idealism and materialism were mostly the outcome of power struggles and social antagonisms.

In fact, all that now remains of those disputes is a confused tangle. The old obstinacy and militancy survive only in the ideology of the Soviet sphere. The indifference that prevails in western philosophy with respect to that elementary dispute often forces Soviet philosophers in particular to invent idealist systems, otherwise they wouldn't have anyone to fight with. At the same time, everything is topsy-turvy. In practice, eastern society comes up with far more idealistic projects than western society. All the great plans for creating Communist society were pure idealism, and even now idealistic notions are fostered about the transformation of people according to a preconceived model: appeals are made to various eternities, in practice dialectics is denied, and propaganda is based on unshakeable, unchanging, and literally sacred principles. It seems paradoxical, but such paradoxes are frequent in history.

From my own reading I gained the impression that Marx himself was much more tolerant than his pupils and epigones when it came to the conflict between idealism and materialism. Naturally, he indulged in many of the impertinences that were customary in 19th century polemics, but otherwise I got the impression that these days he would have cut a poor figure as a foot soldier in the fight against the "idealist world view." Marx banked most of all on historical materialism, which is still cogent. If we leave aside the precise definition of classes according to their relationship to the means of production, Marx's historical materialism threw much light on human history and elucidated above all the basic motivation of all civilizational activity. There can be no doubt that the immediate aim of those historical activities was not self-cultivation but material benefit. It is another matter entirely that this material motivation inspired works whereby humans rivalled the gods. Note that Marx is no longer quoted in practical propaganda these days.

It is not hard for me to imagine how the idea of God as a creator and demiurge of the universe would fit ideally into current Communist ideology. A being like that would sanctify all deeds of the state and state policies, just as he once sanctified the deeds of kings. But it's too late now. The supreme being has been far too long committed to the idealist side, and it wouldn't be easy to switch allegiance to the other camp. Mind you, it would be no paradox if He did, as God has already supported many revolutions and great reforms and continues to, as we know. And I wasn't even thinking of the God of Mohammed.

Everything that the philosophy of history has accumulated concerning this so-called fundamental issue doesn't make very uplifting reading. One doesn't get the impression that those who engaged in furious controversies about what came first, spirit or matter, or whether the world was essentially material or spiritual, were driven by a longing for the truth. From the very outset it was patently obvious that controversies like that were simply spiritual exercises in which the most clever were victorious. The victory was short-lived, however, and off it would start again. Is the resolution of this question really of such importance for humanity? In the end it changes nothing of the reality that people inhabit. Reality is indifferent to both idealism and materialism. It is always one and the same reality, and it looks exactly the same whether we look at it in the belief that it was created by a supreme being or in the belief that it exists eternally and is an end in itself. In either case it is the only reality that people have to live in, and is the source of all their mental stimuli. They can't move out of it because they don't have any other.

3.

But people always sensed that discussions about questions posed in that manner were purely of a speculative nature and conclusions from those discussions were without any proof, even when they were based on the decisions of cardinals or central committees. Though we are reluctant to admit it, we desperately yearn for a proof that would be provided by someone outside our species, someone not human — God or nature itself. But it would have to be absolutely staggering proof, and have all the attributes of scientific proof. So none of your ephemera about miracles, or the laboratory findings of the Lepeshinskys, or the parapsychologists, and so forth. The history of mankind is permeated with the never-ending desire for such proof. People have always pressed God to give a final proof of His existence. Yet they don't want it to happen simply within the realm of theological speculation; the most convincing proof would be if God came on every television channel in the world and spoke to His people as He still did in the Old Testament. But nothing of the kind happens. There is nothing outside of us humans capable of confirming our observations, our truths, or our beliefs. There is a similar longing for non-divine corroboration. Hence the popularity of parapsychology, communicating with spirits, and the like. I suppose some extraterrestrial civilization in the cosmos would supply the most realistic fulfilment of this longing, but even that doesn't come. Humans have apparently been around for millions of years and so far there has not been one single objective confirmation of their most fundamental assertions about the world.

This is ample reason for the nervousness that has accompanied humankind since it became aware of this yearning for proof. It is enough for the humblest object in our surroundings to affirm itself as something more than just what people take it to be, that it exists in and of itself. It could be a little pebble, a flower, an atom of hydrogen, or a single electron freed from its orbit. But we pine in vain for such a materialization of our knowledge. Faust was ready to sacrifice his soul for it.

Human knowledge is based on convention. Basically, all elementary knowledge, which no one would ever think of doubting, is also based on convention. People simply decided that they would call a particular fact of reality by an agreed name and from then on have imagined the selfsame thing by that name. Such a convention undoubtedly suited people's practical needs. In fact, the whole of human civilization was built on that convention. With its help people were able to penetrate the mysteries of nature, the core of matter, and even the nearest reaches of the universe. But we still lack that proof. We ourselves confirm everything we assert, but we don't know whether it is the longed-for Truth. You, Petr, know better than I how some of our experiments with matter run into problems when they take place at the limits of their measurability, how matter slips through our fingers and at one moment is one thing and another something else. We experience similar difficulties when we try to discover some order in the cosmos that would suit our requirements and also contain some harmony.

Reality lies before our eyes, it is all around us, we can touch it with our hands. People have been examining it for centuries with every possible instrument, using it and harnessing it for their needs. And yet we cannot say for sure what it is like. Philosophers have divided reality up and given it names. Everywhere there are things and concepts, substances and phenomena, heavy atoms of the body and light atoms of the spirit, parts and wholes, qualities and quantities, monads and *Dinge an sich*, movement and stasis, and heaven knows what else besides. However, all we have available in this respect is simply the outcome of our mental exercises. So far that voice from on high has yet to be heard, and the objects around us are as silent as they were a million years ago. Still we humans are the only ones in the entire universe to observe, reflect, ask questions, and grope our way.

At this point I ask myself whether all this speculative effort to attain some objective truth is not simply the result of vanity, a remnant of the mythological longing to be like the gods and our inability to quietly accept defeat. After all, it has always been simply a matter of finally accepting that we are the ones who will have to dream up objective proof of the truth of our philosophical axioms. We haven't the ability to break out of our humanity like moths out of a chrysalis and shout, "Hurrah, now I see everything objectively." Man will never become a god that way, and that's the heart of the matter. I don't see why such an admission should necessarily give rise to a general sense of inferiority. Human civilization, everything mankind has achieved in the battle with nature, was based on that practical philosophical convention about reality as a fairly reliable soil on which to live. That convention, from which all speculative and quarrelsome extremes are eliminated, can accommodate everything that matters. Reality conceived in such a practical fashion is propitious for science and everything else that helps create human civilization, and maybe even God views such doings with a sympathetic eye. But this successful praxis in no way verifies the objectivity of our knowledge, as Marx thought. All it confirms is the enormous usefulness of that philosophical convention in which we've made our homes. So, in this area, there is no need for anything to be disturbed, and everything can go on happily working the same way.

What ought to be done away with, however, is the vanity with which many people play god and make a law of "objective reality." Such people proclaim some perception of reality to be "objective" without having the slightest proof of its objectivity. In some individual branch of science, such an approach would raise doubts at the very outset, but in philosophy it is regular practice. Since no objectivity exists in the world, there can be no objective reality either. Meanwhile, the accent is on the attribute. Denying objectivity is not the same as denying reality. I simply maintain that reality is only what we know about it. That there is no reality apart from human reality. Or maybe there is, but we are incapable of judging it other than from our human perspective. All we can judge is what we have taken in, what we have appropriated with our senses and reason, through common praxis and social living. Of itself this is an enormous achievement and is no reason at all for any feelings of inferiority. On the contrary, we should rather be proud of the potentialities offered us by our sensory and mental endowment.

In this respect we have even more before us than behind us; we have work for millions of years to come. But that doesn't entitle us to believe that one day we will cross the threshold and the world will appear in all its objectivity, all its extra-human significance. We cannot assume that reality can be wooed like a woman and that after much hesitation it will one day relent and all mysteries will be effaced. In its researches, modern science often comes to the conclusion that the greater the effort which it makes to woo that woman, the more she will be astounded by the extent of its inalienable mysteries. Until we manage to step out of ourselves, and that is something which, as far as I know, has not been accomplished even in science fiction, we won't be capable of objectivity. However extensive it is, as described by people over thousands of years, reality as a whole is still only human reality, or anthropoid/humanoid reality, if you prefer.

It is pointless here to pose the question how this human reality differs from objective reality independent of humans. We aren't able to answer this question, since we have nothing to compare it with; we know nothing about objective reality. When in ordinary speech, or even in the language of scholarship, we refer to something as objective reality, it is still human reality. No reality can escape these anthropoid clutches. Such human affirmation is not just an attribute of our knowledge, it is an attribute of reality itself.

Of course one could object that I am only saying in another way the same thing as the Solipsists, who in extreme cases refused to acknowledge the reality behind their backs. But you'll have noticed, boys, that in my arguments so far I have not made use of any of the favorite sensory illusions and other evidence of the fallibility of sensory perception. The points I make about reality have very little in common with sensory perception. Even reality that it is not perceived directly is also human reality, since it is contained within human reality, which is again part of our human reality. It's hardly necessary to develop it further; nothing of reality is banished by closing one's eyes, because everything is part of my own reality via other human realities. Our planet rotates in the universe with its blue gleam, but it only speaks to us in our own language. The only objective account of it would have to come from alien eyes observing it from other stars, if such eyes exist. Just as we are captives of this corner of the universe in which our planet moves, so the universe is a captive of our reality. So much for objectivity.

4.

At this stage of deduction we could speculate on whether human reality is mankind's collective property or is instead a conglomerate composed of billions of purely individual realities. I assume that caution and moderation are in order in this respect. Certainly there exists something like collective experience, a general awareness, a basic aggregate of information about reality. That aggregate includes fundamental facts, such as: humans are mortal, the earth rotates around the sun, and a molecule of water comprises two atoms of hydrogen and one of oxygen. But that is hardly enough for us to concede the existence of one single reliably definable reality. As an entity, humankind does not have two common eyes or one common brain, which would take in the whole of human reality. Moreover, apart from what I named, there are not many more things whose definition would be agreed on readily by everyone.

There is no evidence that reality is the same for all people. Besides, you'll recall that I based these speculations on the distressing discovery that two people can possess two diametrically opposed realities preventing them from understanding each other. No, speculation about some collective human reality would immediately get bogged down in insoluble contradictions.

I simply have to reconcile myself with the thought that human reality only appears in individual forms, and what our realities have in common is the result of people's living together, working together, and constantly striving to reconcile individual realities. If this weren't the case, mankind would not have a history full of wars and tribal hostility and conflict — essentially a history of misunderstanding. No less disheartening is people's present inability to reach a common definition of even the most basic needs. War could be defined, for instance, as an attempt by one part of humanity to foist its reality on another part of humanity. In Europe alone, disputes about reality were constantly on the agenda even though the European nations lived in fairly similar circumstances. When two entirely different realities confronted each other, such as the European and the native American, it literally resulted in the annihilation of an entire race of people. Better not think how the confrontation of two cosmic civilizations might turn out.

There are no grounds to attribute to people a single common reality and flirt with the notion that a collectively verified reality is akin to objective reality. You yourselves could provide plenty of evidence to show the deep differences between the realities of various nations and social groups and how that differentiation leads to the isolation of human beings. I can recall the deformations that resulted from speculations about social consciousness based on Marx's unclear directions. In the textbook concept of social consciousness, the whole of human reality was cut in two by the class sword, so that none of the antagonistic classes should have anything in common with the rest. A Russian linguist, who is remembered by almost no one today, actually divided language along those lines. His name was J.N. Marr, and he was the leading philologist of the nineteen-fifties. The fruits of those attempts to unify human reality on the basis of national, class, or racial affinities have been far from encouraging, even though their motivation was a desire to foster knowledge of the world. The trouble is that, because of human nature, the simplest solutions are the hardest to accept. For reasons of inertia, our entire experience resists the idea that human reality is individual, and so apart from the billions of separate realities, we have no tangible evidence of any other. Nonetheless, it is the only solution that satisfactorily answers all doubts, while also unifying the previous experience and respecting the image of the world that emerges from modern developments in the natural sciences.

5.

So what is there to prevent us from accepting the view that emerged long ago, that the single human being is the world, that with a human being a new world is born and then dies with it? It is a view that has been formulated on many occasions in all possible ways. What prevents us most likely is moderation, a fear of blasphemy, respect for the absolute, the towering supremacy of nature, respect for the mysteries of divine counsels and the mysteries of the idea that has no bounds, not to mention the mysteries of such concepts as time, infinite space, and the like.

Such fear is needless, however, as we commit no blasphemy by accepting the notion that the only reality is human reality. We don't even do away with the enormous weight of the universe and the fearsome dictatorship of nature, let alone the mysteries of the metaphysical world. We simply maintain that they are part of anthropoid reality and we are only able to perceive them in terms of that reality. Thus the world remains intact, and we simply appropriate it and make it increasingly our own and refuse to argue about the nature of things that lie outside human reality.

Notice that nature itself does not foist anything on us in "objective" wrapping. In that respect it is totally impassive; it does not harangue us and try to impose any of its truths on us. It simply observes what we do with it. We control natural phenomena by taking possession of them and classifying them as part of our reality. We take things out of impassive nature and appropriate them by giving them names, for instance. That primitive act humanizes reality. By learning its first word, a child orders its reality. And the physicist whose observation takes him into a world where elementary particles are created or destroyed is actually doing the same thing. The enormous difference between the child's reality, which is simply filling itself with first impressions, and the reality of the atomic physicist is only quantitative. I picture human experience as a sort of spherical space that can expand to enormous proportions. In this sense the child's experience is like a tennis ball, while the adult's experience is bigger than the earth, but both those human realities are the same in terms of their nature.

To speak of human reality in terms of a sphere is a primitive model for the sake of argument, but at least it conveys the idea of the quantitative character of that reality. The quantitative differences between the contents of those spheres are naturally enormous. But their qualitative differences are even greater. I have to admit at this point that I have problems finding a model to convey the qualitative differences within anthropoid reality. One could maybe speak in terms of some kind of structure within that spherical space. That structural difference could consist of unequal density; one could think of places with thinner or thicker fabric, bands of light and dark, places where the material of the structure is integrated to varying degrees. But I leave that up to your own imaginations.

It's even harder to envisage a model to demonstrate how that structural diversity is dependent on the owner of that particular reality. I'll go further into this later. For the time being I would simply stress that this spherical space of human experience is only clearly visible from within, and no external observation can be objective. That's the only thing we can be sure of — that objectivity is ruled out.

I realize that what I maintain about anthropoid reality sounds terribly categorical, but these days I am not even able to conceive of reality without human beings. I find repulsive the very concept of objectivity. Whenever I read in the press about some institution, composed naturally of representatives of the human race, reaching an objective decision on something, it makes me feel sick. But I also regard as inappropriate those everyday references to devices that objectively register, record, measure, etc. After all, they are devices made by human beings in terms of their reality. Even the very significance of such apparatus is only intelligible in human terms. Humans created by a machine and leading a separate existence cut off from their creator is felt to be one of the supreme absurdities. It is the kind sci-fi authors enjoy playing with, whereby they have some abandoned automaton play this absurd role: a damaged robot cut off from its program, or any similar device functioning meaninglessly somewhere in the universe, recording and transmitting information that no one is listening to. Where such scenes are well written, the reader has a ghastly sense of the automaton's despair and the absurdity of its existence. Visions of robots in such a predicament are not even utopian any longer. All those space probes intended to observe the outer planets of our solar system fly deeper into the universe and maybe still live and record the wind of distant stars. But for what purpose? What sense has it without human contact?

Of course this is simply one example, and one could find any number of similar ones. I would merely add that if we exclude people from reality, then the whole world becomes deaf and blind and ends up in the pathetic situation of those abandoned automatons.

6.

I'm fairly relieved to abandon that line of argument. After all, you'll find plenty like it in the philosophical literature, and here I can only rely on my memory. A well-informed natural scientist would find far better arguments. And I confess quite freely that all my speculations are concerned chiefly with the reality of ordinary human life and the sum of those realities as a social phenomenon, i.e., the reality that has been riven with contradictions for years and whose description would defy systems of measurement and so-called objective research.

Is it possible to calculate to what extent the reality of two individuals in a cross-section of ordinary everyday life coincide? It's first light, for instance. Six o'clock, because the radio has just given the time. You turn on the tap and water comes out. You light the gas and in a moment the water boils and you pour it over the tea leaves. The tea scorches your mouth while it's hot. The radio is switched on with the turn of a knob and the bus for work leaves at half past six.

All that, in a variety of forms and with a thousand additions, is what constitutes everyday human reality. In many individual details that reality is common to many millions of human beings. And those individual human beings perform faultlessly as part of that everyday reality, reliably carrying out the various tasks associated with it. Few put an empty kettle on the gas, and no one will try switching on the radio by pulling out the aerial. Not many leave the house in their carpet slippers, and no one goes out naked. So far, in terms of basics, the realities of many people are almost identical. For a short while we have the feeling that reality is the same for everyone because it dictates that we leave the house properly dressed.

But let us imagine that two people — neighbors, for instance and both white — look out the window at the same moment that morning. They gaze up at the sky, and both agree that the sun has risen because it is day. But is it the same sun for both of them? Maybe for one of them the sun is simply a symbol of eternal motion — a cosmic clock, a lantern, a practical device that saves electricity, a source of pleasant warmth. In reality, the sun won't mean any more to that first individual in his half-awake state. The second individual, however, bows yoga-fashion to the sun as a source of life. In his reality the sun is a fiery star that has appeared above the horizon because the earth has turned on its axis. For the second individual, the sun has, in addition to its usual meaning, a significance that is physical, poetical, mythological, etc. It could also be a golden chariot drawn by four pairs of horses.

So where is the objective reality between those two people? Is it between them, above them, or possessed by some third person? Who possesses it, in fact? Clearly no one. That morning, the sun is simply two human realities miles apart. The problem is few people feel like indulging in such speculations first thing in the morning. Were we to let those two individuals argue about what the sun meant to them, we would set them at loggerheads and send them off to work in a thoroughly bad mood at the thought of how two people can disagree about such a simple matter as the rising sun.

I hope I've expressed myself clearly enough to show that it is not a new version of Berkeley's old game with pink clouds and disputes about the primary and secondary quality of things. What distinguishes the suns of our two individuals is something infinitely more substantial. It's not just a question of the senses or the differing ability of the eyes and skin of different individuals to perceive the selfsame objective phenomenon. The difference between the two suns is not a matter of different sensitivity but of the different structure of the realities they possess. It is the difference between two worlds. We have already agreed that they are neighbors, both white and both inheritors of European civilization. What would happen if we compared two such banal realities as possessed by two individuals from two very different corners of our planet, such as an American housewife and an Australian aboriginal chief? All we'd need then would be for someone to try and prove which reality was nearest to the sun's objective reality! We'd then have total confusion.

The instance of the sun has all the advantages and drawbacks of such examples, and I deliberately avoid questions of apparent differences in terms of color and temperature, or whether the morning sun is beautiful or ugly, sad or cheerful as viewed by the two imaginary individuals. We are used to this fact and take into account that things around us don't have the same color for each of us and that we don't have the same perception of our surroundings. We tolerate as something quite normal that on one and the same morning one person will go out wearing a fur coat while someone else will leave for work in just a light jacket. We are used to the fact that we all have a different mood in the morning, that some welcome the day with eager and sparkling eyes while others blink with regret as soon as they open their eyes, such as in this prison for instance. But we are not used to thinking that each day we wake up to our reality only, that our neighbor is waking up to another reality, and even that the reality of our dreams is also different.

As I said before, we are afraid to admit it out of fear of Nature, but also out of fear of some possible breakdown in the world of our habits, out of fear that the bus will stop running as it should because the driver inhabits a different reality from ours. We have the feeling that it could mean the end of much of what we regard as natural, that the realization of the difference between the realities we inhabit could undermine the ordinariness of our day. So we are pleased to find that the sun rises on the dot according to astronomical forecasts, because it is a source of security, the basis of objectivity. At that moment we forget that for many individuals the sun hasn't risen and won't rise again, such as those who died in the night, or just before dawn, which is supposed to be more common. A million suns were born and died in a single day. Nevertheless, we assume that it is always one and the same sun, although we are unable to prove it.

I keep on trying to make the point that this line of argument leads to something more substantial than mere references to the unreliability of the senses, differences of moods and feelings, opinions and world views, everything we're accustomed to respect. My two cellmates are currently arguing about whether the mashed peas we had for lunch were edible or not. For want of other amusement it has gone on for quite a while already, and it's more in jest than for real. If I were to tell them that the reason they can't agree is because their taste buds are quite different, I expect they'd accept the explanation without demur. But were I to tell them that the mashed peas in their mess tins were different, they'd stop talking to me and think I'd lost my reason. But it's a fact, nonetheless. The mashed peas were from two different realities. How reluctant we are to accept the most natural explanations.

Every confrontation with contrasting human realities, particularly when it occurs abruptly, is a rather painful experience. When we reflect on the fact that we each have our own spherical space that we inhabit, and that these spaces resemble each other only in terms of the basic accoutrements, we experience a certain atavistic discomfort. It aches like a loss of security, like expulsion from paradise. My feeling is that it's chiefly this pain, this painful fear of their world falling to pieces, that stops people accepting the simple explanation of daily confrontations with differing human realities. It is in fact nothing but the pain associated with every disillusionment. People lose their illusions over and over again throughout their lives, so one more shouldn't be any big deal. However, such losses can also bring joy and relief, particularly to the bravest among us. So in this case, it shouldn't be any great tragedy, either.

The banal example of the morning sun naturally does not illustrate all aspects associated with differences between the most ordinary of human realities. The gulf between individual realities is going to widen when we move from banal examples to more complex situations. For instance, we could have our randomly chosen individuals look out the window one morning at a crowd rushing off to a May Day rally. Even before we've had time to give it much thought we can already appreciate how enormously different will be the realities that parade before the eyes of our two observers. Even if we knew nothing about them, even if we could only judge by their facial expressions, we could bet our bottom dollar that each of them will be seeing something quite different. The reason is, of course, that now they are no longer observing some elementary component of our reality, such as the sun, but something infinitely complex, a social phenomenon that is anthropomorphized by its very make-up. However, let's give those two randomly-chosen individuals a break and compare, Milan, the few lines you wrote in your letter of May 1, for instance, with the radio or television commentary of the same day, and which, even here in prison, I know by heart. Can that contrast in an ordinary description of two events be simply the result of different opinions or even different political attitudes? It can't be! The difference is far more fundamental. It is a difference between two realities, which had diverged much earlier due to different historical experiences and life experience in general. Precisely because it is a social phenomenon, we are suddenly much more willing to admit that no objective reality of the May Day rally exists. How could such objectivity be expressed? In the statistics about those who attended, the number of flags, or the rate of slogan shouting in front of the main platform? No one could seriously think so. And yet I am aware that somewhere in the appropriate quarters someone is putting together an evaluation of the May Day rally. An "objective evaluation," I must stress once again.

We discover that "objective reality" immediately starts to crumble in our fingers if we try to extract from it an even more social phenomenon. In that respect the May Day example is still too banal. What if instead we were to consider wars, ideologies, revolutions, coups d'état, and mass movements, and tried to impose an objective order on such phenomena? I can already sense our hair starting to stand on end at the thought of such "objectivity." And yet it happens day in day out. Every organ of the mass media pours out guaranteed objective news, guaranteed objective endeavors, and similar humbug. But all that objectivity is manufactured by people, and is the fruit of their interests, attitudes, and viewpoints, that is, their own reality through which all that objective blather is filtered.

But let us leave that line of argument. It occurs to me you've known all about this for a long time anyway. It will be much more fun to take a look at reality released from the clutches of objectivity, as we consider reality as the individual property of every human being.

7.

I compared human reality to a spherical space in the middle of which we each stand. These spaces are so heterogeneous, and at first sight are filled with so many different things and structured in so many different ways, that we gaze on them in dumb amazement. When and how did all that wealth get in there? In this connection it immediately occurs to us that some of that human reality might have been there at the very outset. Was it simply a bare plain, or was there something growing there already? It's a prickly question and it relates, as you know, to Kant and other philosophers who colonized that plain from the very beginning with witches, fates, immortal souls, moral laws, and so on. But if I am to abide strictly by the logic of the evidence given so far in respect of human reality, I am obliged, whether I like it or not, to assume that at the beginning, before birth, there is an empty plain. Bare, white, cheerless, like the primal matter out of which everything was going to be created — although I know nothing about that first moment. Maybe it happens long before birth, long before the first cry and the first time the eyes open in the uterine darkness, when the first links take place in the initial chaos. Maybe the basic plain of reality already begins to take shape at that moment as a rough design for the eventual structure. And so as not to annoy Kant, it could be that the genetic design in question also comprises moral precepts and other basic requisites of humanity: the need for faith, God, love, and so on. Whether the plain is bare or something already stands on it, complex reality only starts to grow thereon in the course of life.

It is important to regard it all as an act of creation. Reality does not build itself; humans are constructing it all the time. The child that opens its eyes for the first time to receive the first inverted image of the world is a bit like that first cosmic constructor, because, be it as it may, in spite of the enormous material supplies available to it in its surroundings from the very beginning, that defenseless child will become the direct creator of its own reality. And it will work tirelessly, starting at the first moment of its existence and not stopping until the moment of its death, that cosmic catastrophe, when everything returns to its original state.

It strikes me that the most important and also the most beautiful feature of human reality thus conceived is its creative character. What human beings are provided with at the outset is only building material — bricks and mortar — from which they must build reality in their own image, as God once did with the world. Unlike him, however, they don't work just six days but their entire lifetimes. They definitely have more time for the task. My feeling is that the whole mystery of divine creation is essentially a poetic description of the creation of human reality.

The nearest we get to understanding the entire process is when we analyze works of art and particularly works of literature. The reality of a work of art — a painting, a sculpture, a poem — is just as authentic as any other reality. In fact it fulfils every age-old dream and is the creator of its own reality. This understanding — particularly in respect of literature — is now widely accepted, although in our country there still survives the ludicrous notion that people are simply a mirror, a reflective surface, providing a more or less truthful reflection of objective reality. A Bulgarian academician of blessed memory once wrote several thick tomes about the theory of reflection, and it made particularly cheerless reading. Although the theory was based on a number of quotations from Lenin, it reduced the artist to a passive mirror, which does its best to reflect reality according to some objective formula, in our case, the formula of socialist realism.

But that was more of a remark in passing. Anthropoid reality is the outcome of creative activity. We know that from our experience. People create their reality with their entire being and use every part of their personality in the process. Certainly in the first place they use their senses, but that is not all. An important role in the creation of one's own reality is played by borrowed experience, which is an enormous source of material. Then comes feeling, intellect, and all the transcendental resources peculiar to human beings. This means that the differences in the realities of individual human beings are not the result of difference in sensory perception; people have any number of available tools for creating reality; nature has equipped them better than any other living creature. All these tools, particularly those whose function transcends mere sensory perception, are also a prerequisite for the creative act of creating reality.

To understand human reality as the result of creative activity is as important as the entire basic reasoning. What we are developing here is actually the old idea that people confront the world not as a passive recorder of events — some kind of recording machine — but instead as an active conqueror of the world. Man is a bully who appropriates everything; he's like a thief who steals everything he sees and only when he gets it home starts to think of what to do with it. Some landscape artists work in that fashion. They sit down in a landscape, look around them, make a few sketches, and then create their picture in the studio. The landscape only comes into being with that picture; only then is it reality. In one letter to me Milan writes about nature always being there. He has in mind the forests and meadows he runs through. He says that nature is always waiting and that we have to go and find it in order to be aware of it. That is precisely the point I'm making. That is the creative act whereby we create our reality. We appropriate the beauty of nature, for instance, by running through it for fifteen kilometers with tongues lolling out, or when we encroach on it actively in any other way, whether as plowmen, surveyors, tourists, mushroom pickers, or as builders of dams, railway lines, motorways, or nuclear power stations, which are now regarded as destructive of nature. But that's another issue.

However, nature does not wait for us in the form we find it. We have no idea what it is like until we enter it. Only then does it become part of our reality. We don't know precisely what was there before, even though nature existed as part of our reality — but in another quality, not in the quality of direct access. Nature constantly exists in our reality, even in the dark and in our dreams, and in a prison cell. It is a reality created out of our own memories, no matter how old they are. Memories of our entire lives. This reality of nature is also everything we have read about it or seen on the screen, everything other people have told us about it, everything to which we have had access. Direct contact with nature is a new reality that is laid onto the old, thus creating a complex structure. In this way we actually incorporate each new separate piece of knowledge, layering old and new components of our reality, turning them over and refashioning them.

Our subconscious recalls this process. You know the feeling, don't you, when you come to a place you have only previously known from literature or hearsay and all of a sudden direct perception and received experience overlay one another? Karel Čapek muses about this in his English Letters, for instance, and I have a similar recollection. Before I first visited London, that city was already part of my reality. I had created it out of postcards, films, literature, thrillers, and so on. London was a reality without my ever having seen it. When I eventually stood on Waterloo Bridge, like Karel Čapek I had the feeling I had already been there some time in another life, that it was simply a return, and I was looking again at the river and the Houses of Parliament. But it was actually my old and new realities of London intermingling, merging, and influencing each other. That combination still lives on in me, and I expect there will be another layering if I ever get the opportunity again some time to stand on that bridge and look around me.

Within each individual these various layers of reality are in constant motion, tossing about and changing and giving rise to new realities corresponding to new times, new circumstances, and new states of mind. After every external impulse, every new glance, every new shot on television, every news item on the radio, and while reading every new book, our reality is reshaped. It is thus a permanent act of creation that continues from birth to death. It is as if we were writing a book non-stop and describing things around us, reflecting the changing seasons and changes within ourselves — in joy and in sadness. However, this all happens automatically. We are accustomed to this activity as an attribute of our humanity. We learn to do it as easily as a baby learns to invert the image of the world that it receives with its eyes. We are "condemned" to do so, to use the existentialist expression. We have to do so in order to live. Because only by this appropriation of reality are we able to make head and tail of it and use it to satisfy all the needs we have as living creatures. As far as we know, we are the only creatures in the universe to be equipped with this creative ability. Were it not so, everything would be immediately different.

8.

In view of current psychological knowledge, I shouldn't think it would be hard to describe almost precisely the way in which the spherical space of reality that surrounds us is filled from childhood, to observe how it expands with the addition of newer and newer material, how structures are created within it, how colors merge or are defined, how, quite simply, a world is created out of primal chaos. Even so, we will hardly ever be capable of describing the reality of the very beginning, the world of the newborn baby, who looks with a pure but empty gaze. Maybe it is only a reality of light and shade, and in the middle of it God — the mother. There seems to be no doubt about this central figure of initial reality. Countless defects of awareness are now shown to be the result of defects in the relationship between mother and child. Indeed, are these defects not defects of reality? In the final analysis, all defects in the behavior of human beings take the form of some defect in the creation of reality. Such distortions can simply result from the fact that at the very beginning the child's reality lacked the mother figure, regarded, let's say, as the basic prop of the entire structure of reality to be created.

As the human being moves away from the first months of life, the act of creating reality continues in many different ways, and it is much easier for us to reconstruct and imagine it. It is nonetheless still the child who creates it. The child is the lightning builder, and we are overcome with amazement when we realize the enormous creative power hidden within it, how its brain, like a gigantic computer, processes with ant-like diligence an unending stream of data and transforms it into a picture of the world. There is no doubt that by the age of three, a child's reality is of respectable proportions and has markedly individual characteristics. When I remember the two of you when you were about five years old, I can still recall how amazed I was that you could be so different and how your five-year-old individual realities could have such distinct characteristics that one could tell them apart at first glance.

Take children's drawings, for instance. Artists, psychiatrists, pedagogues and parents will all find something in them. They are always, however, a simple reproduction of children's reality, and for all their complexity, colorfulness and emotional saturation, they only contain what can be conveyed by the simple technical tools of pencil or colored crayons. If we could sit down inside a child's reality as in a cinema and project a colored film about it, our amazement would be infinitely greater.

The senses undoubtedly play a primary role in the construction of reality. Reality itself is created from what the eyes see, the ears hear, the skin touches, the nose smells, and the tongue tastes. Yet one could imagine as well how the human being's other resources also take part in the construction of reality almost simultaneously with this sensory activity. There is an especial ability to receive reality via a third party, i.e., the ability to learn. In this way the child adopts received reality, such as the reality of its parents, its siblings, its friends, its teachers, and so on. This process of reception is even more complex than sensory perception. After all, the whole question of education is bound up with this process. We know plenty about the enormous stumbling blocks, obstacles and hardships that strew the route from the alien reality to the building site on which the child builds its first castles and tunnels. I deliberately call it a building site, because education takes place at a time when everything is still unfinished. The child does not watch impassively while others build its reality. At the very outset my assumption was that human beings all have a genetically determined individual building plan, with drawings of the foundations and fine lines indicating links. This blueprint simply resists any interference from alien builders. This is what often explains the total failure of educators. Herein lies the enormous disappointment that followed the great hopes of transforming the world. I refer to the hopes that the human being was born as a tabula rasa, and education, if properly directed, was capable of writing on this clean page a list of the noblest qualities and deeds and thus create an angel from every individual. Incidentally, as you know from my writings about utopias, that notion was the cause of the failure of all utopian goals, including the goal of creating a new, socialist, or even communist man. All the sciences that now deal with the child are likely capable of describing the sphere of influences that affect the character of the individual, in other words, the entire complex process whereby personal human reality is created. But though we might describe it accurately, we are unable to explain the fact that identical influences in identical circumstances give rise to two human beings whose realities are quite different. It would appear that human realities differ from each other like the whorls on our fingertips. Even when we are aware that genetic information is written with billions of variations, we are nevertheless lost in wonder at the law that does not allow even two people among the billions on earth to be the same, or to have two totally matching realities. It looks as if everything around us, which is rooted in the laws of nature, resists tooth and nail any objectivization or leveling down. We will never be capable of creating a copy of people and their realities in the manner horrifyingly described by Aldous Huxley. At most we could find a common denominator for a select number of human realities and perhps draw from them an arithmetical average, even though this would also be our own fiction and have nothing to do with objective reality.

There is no point in rebelling against the natural tendency to diversity. On the contrary, we should be pleased about it and quietly smile at the difficulties it creates for educators, politicians, and indeed anyone who would sooner hold sway over statistical averages rather than diverse individuals.

When we look back on our childhood and youth it is not hard to specify the circumstances and influences that contributed most significantly to our reality. We are able to point to a particular voice, book, or event, say, that ensured that one particular corner of our reality looks the way it does. We can remember one or even ten such experiences, but we are unlikely to search out the enormous number of additional influences, both crucial and of minor significance, that also helped shape our reality. We must resign ourselves to the fact that it is probably impossible to create a mathematical model to express the effect of those influences. The two of you shared equally in each major event of our family life. You were with us in the same places, read the same books, heard the same advice and rebukes and literally ate out of the same dish. And yet you both know how disparate your two realities are. It would seem that people have greater immunity to unification than to viral infections. In the course of life, human reality is created in all those virtually indefinable ways. It would almost be more appropriate to speak in terms of shaping human reality, rather than shaping the human personality, as the extent and structure of that reality determine the dimensions of the human individual.

9.

But if it is the case that every human being has its own particular reality, then the old problem of human communication appears in a rather different light. It's an old problem, because there has always been an awareness of the enormous obstacles standing in the way of human understanding. In recent times science has made enormous efforts to study those obstacles and has come up with hundreds of reasons for the lack of human communication. There is now a remarkable degree of scepticism about the whole issue and people are often regarded as dumb creatures. Occasionally someone will concede that they are capable of communication, but only about trivia, or that everyone speaks his own particular gibberish and makes no effort to be understood, and he himself doesn't listen to others. But that's nothing new to you.

A lot has been done, for instance, concerning language as a means of communication and its somewhat deceptive mystery has been researched. Modern psychology, sociology, ethnography, pedagogy, and the anthropological sciences in general give rise to similar scepticism. Modern art seems to go out of its way to prove that communication between human beings is impossible. I can still recall from the time when normal literary criticism existed in this country how almost every review of modern fiction ended by saying that the book in question was yet further evidence of human solitude and the impossibility of human communication. Art as a whole fostered the ubiquitous model of human individuals vainly contending with loneliness and gradually discovering that the gulf between them and other people was only growing wider. Every self-respecting filmmaker had to make a film about the impossibility of communication. You've seen plenty of films in this vein, by Fellini, Antonioni, Resnais, Bergman, and others. I can't recall when I first saw Bergman's *Silence* — maybe it was abroad or at some private film show — but I can still remember the shock of it. The whole problem — namely, that people can live side by side without finding a means of communicating — was advanced in the film almost as a philosophical axiom, yet without undermining in any way the film's emotional impact. Nevertheless, I believe that the most terrifying film about the despair of loneliness, the impossibility of conveying one's own anxiety, the sense of being locked inside one's own life, and the inability to call for other people's help would be a film made of Kafka's story about Gregor Samsa turning into a beetle. Who knows, maybe it's already been filmed. When I first read the story many years ago it was like being hit on the head. I can also remember us not so long ago watching together the film version of Camus's *The Stranger*. The fact is, almost the whole of modern art is about loneliness.

When it's not directly about it, then it is at least about the desperate efforts to break through the invisible curtain lowered between the individual and the rest. And I need not recall that the first of the rest is most frequently the wife or husband.

Now I realize it is presumptuous to speak only about modern art in connection with this problem; it was already present in old art. Who was Don Quixote? A typical loner, as Milan Uhde enjoys saying. Pierre Bezukhov is also a solitary madman as he tears about the battlefield or through the flames of Moscow. He watches, but he has long realized that he won't understand. Although he is a Russian patriot, the actions of the French and Russian armies appear to him absurd — but Tolstoy didn't use this expression, as it wasn't yet current.

So I don't believe it to be a purely modern problem. Maybe people have had that hump of loneliness since the days of mammoth hunts. But in those days they had far more important things on their minds than to worry about it in detail. The problem was not unknown to the ancient philosophers, though it was Jesus' outburst on the cross of "Eli, eli, lamma sabaktani" that imprinted it on human awareness. For on the cross he could not even draw comfort from being understood. Even those crucified alongside him mocked him.

Recognition of the fact that each individual human being has his or her own reality seems to bring no relief in the great unrequited longing for communication. It would seem that such a concept of reality actually confirms human beings' eternal loneliness and their inability to achieve total understanding with others. In acknowledging diverse realities we lose all hope. While one might accept the possibility that people from a single objectively existing reality might understand each other, how could people with millions of different realities understand one another? What hope of understanding is there when each human reality is another world?

The logic of such a conclusion is impossible to deny. In such a case comfort comes from a somewhat different mental operation: I have demonstrated many times that all quarrels about truth and the authenticity of perception are artificially created, that they are simply games with conventionally established rules. (I should make clear, however, that I don't say this with any disrespect. Chess is also a game with fixed rules, and what a science that is!) Such games are based on one fundamental rule: reality exists objectively, and with effort we can all achieve precisely the same perception of that reality. The mental shift away from this consists of refusing to recognize the rule while creating others for ourselves on the grounds that the former rule was framed for gods, and whenever people tried to observe it they always ended up in a state of despondency. The same goes for the problem of communication! All the misery of latter-day dissatisfaction stemming from loneliness and the impossibility of communication is also the result of observing the conventional rule. In other words, we are incapable of complete identification within that conventionally-defined objective reality. It is better not to fall prey to that illusion and instead base ourselves on the premise that no two human realities can ever be identical, so all that age-old yearning for total identification and coalescence of the soul is simply false.

You could object that vain yearning would be no less vain or painful were we simply to tell it to get lost, because it is false and should never have come into existence in the first place. Well, for my part I think every loss of illusion is a consolation, but in our case this is not the main thing. We rid ourselves of illusions in order to better appreciate the possibilities of human understanding as well as its limits. We are not losing anything; on the contrary, something is gained. Though we recognize the transcendental nature of such longing for understanding and coalescence, we subordinate it to other rules. We are ridding ourselves of illusions to achieve real understanding.

No two human realities are identical and cannot be so, however devoutly one may wish it. Their different internal structure, their historical background, their genetic makeup, and all their accumulated experience militate against it. That is why not even identical twins can have totally matched realities. This is the basis of it all, not some ancient curse that stands in the way of mutual understanding.

Of course I do not kid myself that by asserting this I have rid the world of that curse. Even the awareness of such a curse is part of human reality, and is consequently no less real. Even the yearning for coalescence remains a part of human reality and is therefore no less obsessive. It provokes deep sorrow and often aggressiveness. For when yearning is not requited in any way, people often try to force others to accept their reality. Yearning is languid, arousing pity and tearing at heart strings, but then the same yearning for understanding often develops into roars, slaps, kicks, and refined torture. Such a slap or a kick expresses a despair that is purely philosophical in origin, even though the expression is unphilosophical. And as we know, the final step in that direction is murder. By killing them we indeed win them over to our reality, as they no longer have any other. However, we shall never receive confirmation of that perfect coalescence. Such a yearning for identification can be just as aggressive as the yearning for truth. People addled by the age-old idea of some universal truth are always seeking doors to the fundamental secret. More often than not they kick them down only to discover that there is nothing behind them, just dusty corners and emptiness. There are plenty of people who break their way into the thirteenth chamber of the human soul only to discover nothing at all.

There is no need to bow to the longing for understanding and intimate discourse between human beings if we recognize that we each live within our own reality. There is nothing to prevent us trying to get to know someone else's reality or to let others have a look at ours. That is, of course, how everything begins! Two realities sniff each other like a couple of dogs. They are delighted to find they are similar in many ways, amazed by unknown things and surprising discoveries. They could also be confused by what they find, but in all events there must be some reaction. The reaction to this alien reality might be antagonism or simply indifference, but more often than not it is interest and sometimes even pleasure, a pleasure that gives rise to friendship, love, genuine communication, and all other positive relations among people. Those positive relations then manage to last if respect for the other reality is maintained and if those involved are capable of suppressing the irrational desire to take possession of the other reality.

What I'm saying, therefore, is that there is nothing wrong with recognizing that no two human realities can be identical. Nothing is lost by it; on the contrary, an irrational obsession is replaced by positive scope for rapprochement and interpersonal communication. We are offered the opportunity to treat others' realities with respect, admiration, tolerance, and all other human virtues. It is a positive opportunity for conscious activity without having to wait for irrational orders from the instincts' HQ.

Communication can take place provided there is goodwill and respect for the architectural characteristics of the other's reality. However, that respect only lays the foundations for meetings. The landscapes of our realities can penetrate and enrich each other; the smell of home cooking wafts through the open windows in both directions. If there is mutual interest, doors to secret rooms are opened, and the paths in the garden lead out to sun-drenched meadows as well as to tenebrous hollows which even the master or mistress of the house fears to visit. On this basis of tolerance, full-scale expeditions to our fellow human beings may be mounted and miracles of genuine understanding experienced.

Every reality is enriched by such encounters, expanding as it absorbs new material. This kind of communication is in fact a condition for the growth of one's own reality. Loss of interest in the reality of others is tantamount to loss of interest in the development of one's own reality. It is a loss of interest in life, in fact.

This is a joyful discovery, isn't it? Communication is possible, and so are understanding and profound harmony. However, such communication is not the unification of elements of objective reality, but the result of offer and acceptance: offering one's own reality and accepting another's. The very concepts of offering and accepting are concepts of ancient rituals. We can enjoy the spaciousness and heterogeneity of the world, its profusion of forms, and accept the realities of others, from astronomers to deep-sea divers.

In our own reality we are all equal. We are all owners and there is no need to envy anyone else. Only in terms of the quality of these realities are we not equal: there are rich and poor, greedy and indolent. However, that inequality, evidently the result of birth and life experience, is simply another incentive to offer and receive. These are ways of becoming rich.

As a result of this mental operation, the old anxiety about loneliness is transformed into loneliness without anxiety. I don't think it's hard to accept that I am alone within my own reality when I know I can welcome guests and pay visits to others. I can amass wealth, in terms of my inner abundance, not an abundance of things. I'm not worried by the thought that when I die my reality dies with me, apart from those facets of it which have migrated to other people.

In general it's satisfying to inhabit one's own territory. It's the only one in which we are absolute rulers. True, it can be invaded by doctrinarians, pedants, and ideologists of objective truths and necessities, capable of saying incredible things such as: subjectively you meant well but objectively you're an enemy and deserve the gallows. Nevertheless it's up to us: they may stand on some tree stump and spout whatever they like, but we don't have to change a single footpath or fell a single tree in our landscape on their account. The whole secret of freedom is hidden in that landscape. But this is another story.

10.

So you see, it wasn't too difficult on the basis of that model to create a whole slew of instances from life showing a hundred forms of human communication and intercourse of every kind, as D.T.[1] would say. But I'm already rushing off to another application: the social application. After all, this is where the concept of reality as objective reality independent of people created havoc at the very dawn of history, and it still isn't finished doing so.

For heaven's sake, don't go off with the idea that I want to make a

---

1. Dominik Tatarka: 1913-1989, Slovak writer who achieved fame with his novel *Demon of Consent* (1963). Because of his opposition to the 1968 invasion and the subsequent neo-Stalinist restoration, he was banned from publishing. He was among the first signatories of Charter 77.

revolution. I wouldn't want to create the impression that a mere abstract mental operation — equivalent, say, to that proverbial inversion of the world — could have a fundamental influence on real history and is responsible for the continuing barbarity. Human reality is not a mere abstract product of the brain like Mr. Kelly's Sirael.[2] It is something concrete and material; it causes pain, it agitates, egging people on to deeds and crimes, actions of every kind, and at a certain point it matters little whether they realize they are acting as part of their own reality or some objective reality. So we're forced to admit, alas, that the history of mankind probably wouldn't have been much different if people had known at the outset that all those great ideas that they enthused about or had foisted on them were not divinely inspired or an objective necessity, but instead were the outcome of human experience. Admittedly history would be much more transparent and instructive (although it is my pessimistic finding that people are incapable of learning lessons). Whatever the case, it would have been obvious rather soon that many great ideas simply masked people's base, materialistic, and instinctive motives of which they were ashamed. (These days they are not even ashamed, as you've no doubt discovered.)

In those cases where people are capable of drawing lessons from history, an awareness of human reality is very useful because it fosters contempt for ideologists of every ilk and for all objectively sanctified ideas. In the light of such contempt history is certainly instructive. Ceremonial costumes are suddenly not so impressive, and ideologies, those real scourges of humanity, don't look so deadly serious. In the final analysis the only real lesson to emerge in connection with human reality is tolerance.

There is no need to go far in search of such a lesson — how about, how about . . . For instance: my dad actually fought in World War I. I used to hear members of the previous generation talk about it and I read lots of books about it, because it was the main subject matter before the

2. A reference to the English alchemist Edward Kelly at the court of the Emperor Rudolf II. Legend has it that Kelly created a beautiful woman, Sirael, whom the emperor could see, but not touch.

second war broke out. Not long ago I re-read *All Quiet on the Western Front*. In the entire book there's nothing about the reasons for the war. No good book ever does provide precise reasons, unless one accepts the division of markets and colonies as the reason. Such explanations do not tell us why the war led to the death of millions of people who couldn't give a damn about markets and knew nothing about any colonies. As I'm in the clink I can permit myself to make totally unscientific assertions, so I maintain that the only explanation for World War I was hatred: the hatred of the Germans for the French, the French for the Germans, the English for the Prussians, the Russians for the Poles and vice versa, the Czechs for the Germans, and so on and so forth. (Though to be totally fair, the Serbians were resisting aggression, and I also concede that many were fighting for freedom, a better world order, the liberation of oppressed nations, and peace.) Essentially, all the motives for going to war were based on prejudice, various opportunistic ideologies, ideological mimicry — in a nutshell, differences of reality. In the French reality the Germans were real and objective enemies and vice versa. But one just can't dismiss the war as the result of human stupidity. The reality itself was idiotic — an accumulation of antagonisms and the inability of nations to reach agreement or understanding. What I'm trying to say is that first of all the situation in which people lived went crazy and then the people inevitably went crazy, too. The realities of the European nations were so diverse that they could no longer live together side by side and were bound to start fighting.

These days everything is much more transparent; as time goes by and history loses its ideological clichés the motives of human actions become clearer. That doesn't apply to everyone, though: whenever I read our newspapers, I get the impression that the opposite is true. The press now perfectly embodies the slogan from *Nineteen Eighty-Four*: "Who controls the past controls the future; who controls the present controls the past." An ordinary item of world news is so ideologically distorted that I chase it away from the very threshold of my reality. Items about past history, on the other hand, emerge from some obscure reality that isn't even on my list, so luckily I can't even place it anywhere. I console myself with the thought that elsewhere in the world there still exists a different sort of press.

Thus my references to greater transparency refer to the history of other countries, not our own, or to the history of the world in general as observed by those who are not under supervision and forced to look from a different perspective. From the latter perspective it is obvious that all ideological motives of historical acts were consecrated by objectivity and would not have been possible without that consecration. Ideologies always had truth on their side, a truth that always derived from some such consecration — it could come from on high, but most importantly it came from objective reality, which verified all the truths of the world. All that remains of most of those truths is dust and ashes. That's why I never much liked the slogan The Truth Will Prevail,[3] because one can never be sure which truth is referred to. All that is needed for decency to prevail in society is respect for the principle that I know from Winston Smith: freedom is the freedom to say two and two is four, and then all else follows. It's an enormous difference. Two times two need not be four in all circumstances, but what is important is the freedom to say it aloud. Freedom is more important than truth. Truth can never be guaranteed, but freedom can.

This is the fundamental lesson that my concept of reality draws with respect to history. However, in accordance with that lesson I cannot force my concept on you or the entire lesson would be annulled. I'd also like to add that I am not mocking devotion to the truth, even to some ideological truth. After all I studied Marx — and even now I can still feel clearly how exhilarating it was to realize that I now held in my hand the key to the entire mechanism of social reality. From that moment I understood that history was moving objectively towards the annihilation of capitalism and the inevitable creation of communism as a realm of freedom. The attraction of such a concept of objectivity is the feeling

---

3. The motto of the Czech state.

of certainty that pervades the soul. The believers simply queue up and are objectively transported to communism. Of course Marx didn't express it that crudely, but in ideology his objectivity was given that hallmark. Besides, it wasn't his idea but Hegel's, who did not base himself on the material conditions of life but on the world soul. It's incredible how, although things here limp, stagger, and stumble along, we still march forward in step with history — objectively and optimistically . . .

The attractiveness of ideologies explains their longevity and capacity for revival. Can anything be "objectively" changed by the realization that it is false to argue in terms of objective social movement, objective truth, and objective reality, because no such objectivity exists and the whole of reality is to be found only in the cosmic space of human beings? That human history is also stored within this reality, and not outside of people in pyramids and archives? That papyrus with some markings on it only begins to operate as history when it falls into the hands of a historian? That society parades before us like that May Day rally of yours and it all depends how we lay claim to it? This is the most treacherous question we could ever ask. Were we to answer it positively we would undermine the foundations of all the previous arguments, because it would be tantamount to admitting that a purely mental operation could affect the behavior of societies as a whole. I have to express myself more circumspectly, something along the following lines:

My answer is that it cannot, although I'd love to believe that by realizing these things people might be more sceptical about those who endlessly trumpet that they know what is eternal, what is irrevocable, what is objective and true, what is or isn't the future of the world, what must be fought for, what is sacred, who is friend and who is foe. It would be a total revolution if people realized that they cannot force other people into an alien reality, if they realized that tolerance and forbearance towards the realities of others — and not only individuals, but also individuals who together constitute a nation or a social group — is simply an assertion that objective reality does not exist and to say so is not treachery, weakness, or appeasement as is still often claimed. Tolerance of the diverse realities that people inhabit would be a beneficial outcome that no revolution has ever achieved in this world.

Let us imagine a world that acknowledged this simple thesis. Were it to draw the appropriate political lessons from it, the world would be quite a nice place to live in. It would be a paradise that tolerated this terrible disharmony and accepted that an American housewife wakes each morning to a different reality than a Soviet lecturer in a museum of atheism, for instance. And it wouldn't matter. In such a world even my interrogator would be transformed into a tolerant individual who would accept that my writings simply reflected the nature of my own reality and were not intended to destroy the state. No, no, let's forget it and not delude ourselves.

It's not healthy to go on about the social applications, it simply leads to needless confusion. Even if tolerance made no progress at all, people could still find enough consolation in their own reality. It's impossible to disregard the barbarity of the reality into which they have been dragged by those with a monopoly of objective truth, because a mere peek into it arouses despair. But if they are strong enough they can preserve the landscape of their reality, even if all that remains of it is a roof to shelter under with their near ones, a few books, and a few logs to keep warm. In the end it's their landscape, and no one can take it away from them.

courtesy of Jiřina Šiklová

Milan Šimečka a few days before his death, September 1990.

courtesy of the Milan Šimečka Foundation

Summer, 1982.

courtesy of Lenka Procházková

Milan Uhde and Šimečka at the cottage, 1983.

courtesy of Jolana Kusá

Tomky, 1986. From the left: Ivan Klíma, Miroslav Kusý, Karel Pecka, Milan Šimečka.

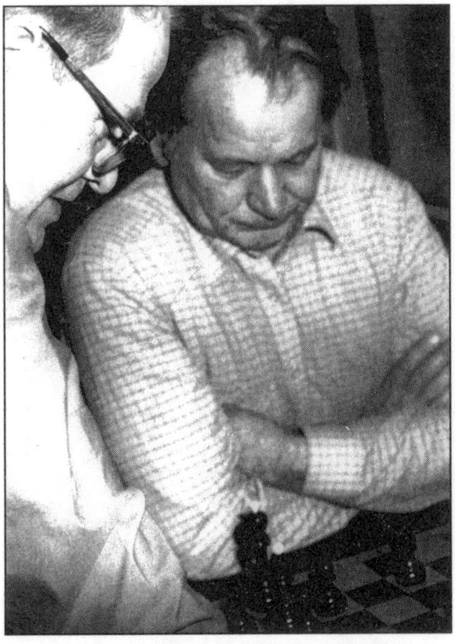

courtesy of Jolana Kusá

With Julius Strinka on Chess Tuesdays at the Kusýs'.

courtesy of Lenka Procházková

An *Obsah* gathering, 1983. From the left: Ludvík Vaculík, Eda Kriseová, Milan Šimečka, Lenka Procházková.

photo by Gerald Turner

With Tanya Turner at Jiřina Šiklová's cottage, 1986.

courtesy of Kritika & Kontext

The Skillings' fiftieth wedding anniversary dinner at Obecní dům, Prague, 1987. From the left: H. Gordon and Sally Skilling, Václav and Olga Havel, Eva and Milan Šimečka.

photo by Gerald Turner

At his cottage in Cyrilov, Moravia, 1987.

courtesy of Jiřina Šiklová

H. Gordon Skilling in Šimečka's office at Prague Castle, summer 1990.

MILAN ŠIMEČKA: A PROFILE[1]

Milan Šimečka was born on March 6, 1930; he died September 24, 1990. His life's pilgrimage, the "creation of one's own reality," from birth till the moment of one's death, the "cosmic catastrophe, when everything returns to its original state" — to use Šimečka's words to define human life — lasted sixty years and six months. I shall try to outline the main features of Šimečka's life and work, as well as his place in independent Czech and Slovak thinking in the second half of the twentieth century. I should also like to help to answer the question concerning who Šimečka was and remains for those who had the good fortune to live part of their lives near him, and especially how one feels affected and changed after reading his work.

He was born in Nový Bohumín. He later described his native region as the Czech tip of Silesia at the river Oder, where people of various nationalities had lived since time immemorial. In 1987 he wrote:

> As a child I was subject to the illusion that the division [into Czechs, Germans, Poles, Jews, and so on] was secondary, that the variety of languages, natures, and origins was considered natural and beneficial, that it prevented nobody from having good relations as a citizen, neighbor, or person. Even now it seems to me that I spent my childhood in authentic internationalism. My aunts, who declared themselves Germans, offered me Sunday cake just as lovingly as my aunts who considered themselves Czechs.[2]

---

1. This profile is an abridged version of "The Great and Small Histories of Milan Šimečka," by Vilém Prečan, translated by Derek Paton, *Kritika & Kontext*, no. 3-4, (1999), pp. 46-71. It was originally written for a conference on Šimečka's life and work (held in Bratislava, September 20, 1991) which was organized by the Milan Šimečka Foundation to mark the first anniversary of his death. The profile was published in *Slovenské pohľady*, January 1992, pp. 17-29, and then in a volume of the conference papers, titled, similarly as the profile, *Velké a malé dějiny Milana Šimečku* (Bratislava, 1992).
2. For Šimečka's childhood see his essay "Cizinci," which was written in August 1987 for inclusion in a publication on relations between Germans and their neighbors. Neither the book nor the essay has ever been published. The manuscript and its German translation are found in the Šimečka Papers, the

He went to elementary school before World War II, during the war, and after it, and, as he himself said, experienced three or four kinds of influence. He provided much revealing information about his childhood and becoming an adult when replying to a questionnaire sent to him by Lenka Procházková in 1985, "What did you do and what did you believe in when you were twenty?":

> Each attempt to approach my youth is accompanied by a feeling of wonder, distance, and of a completely different world. [...] It was a world of a particular historical moment, it was cruel with the simplicity the war left behind, it was overflowing with hope and illusions . . . it stomped its feet and berated us that we had to decide. Today few believe we were forced to decide mainly so that in the next decisive struggle we could die on the right side of history. [...] It was a time of Ayatollahs. [...] The ideological struggle appeared to be absolutely authentic. The weight of history back then appeared to be enormous, menacing, and ominous; it left little space to the ordinary human dimension and impressed urgently on young people, that to listen to mysterious historical laws was far more dignified for a man than to listen to the weary whispering of some outmoded morality.
>
> I see, looking back, what sort of determining factors we were faced with and how frivolously they turned us towards this or that side. I was not endowed with a working-class origin, but I was an orphan, and in that post-war wave of social sentimentality that was almost the same. I lived in the loving care of my sister and was not wanting in anything; the state showered me with its favor. They waived the payment of all fees, I received the largest scholarships, and I met with kind behavior everywhere. I (unlike my sons) was able to study whatever I liked. I reckoned the state was good and that it deserved my thanks. It was not even so much a matter of the money they gave me; rather it was that they had raised my worth in my own eyes. I assumed I was acting honorably when I demonstrated my gratitude by enthusiastically helping to build [the socialist state]. I took part in all the well-known work brigades. Did it

---

Czechoslovak Documentation Centre; originally at Scheinfeld–Schwarzenberg, Germany, the Centre relocated to Dobřichovice outside of Prague in 2000.

ever occur to me that the state was buying my devotion? I would be lying if I said it did. And yet, might not these determining factors have taken the opposite course? If a Roman Catholic charity had looked after me, might I not have become a loyal Catholic? So, this is how we are!

Did I love Big Brother? I suppose so, but with secret and painful reservations. Even today I feel that historical determining factor on my skin. In 1945 I was terribly shocked by the damned war. I had become convinced they wanted to kill me in this war. They shot at me from an airplane, at a fourteen-year-old boy who in a white T-shirt was running through a field. They dropped a bomb on the highway fifty meters in front of me when I was on a bike ride with a girl. I stood gaping with horror at the sight of white bones and the twitching guts of families who were stripped out of their Sunday best by the air pressure from the blast. They killed my mother in a bombing raid, and when, after those thundering blows, I crawled from the cellar into the stench, dust, and wasteland, I covered ten kilometers in a state of shock, and to this day don't know how I got where I ended up. I welcomed the muddy and sweaty Ukrainians from Malinovsky's army with the same feeling as those who write to *Rudé právo* on anniversaries [of the liberation]. I didn't feel grateful to them for liberation (I still didn't understand that); I was grateful to them for having put an end to that horrible thing and because now I wasn't going to die without knowing a woman, which at my age back then seemed like the worst thing that could have happened. If some black Americans from Virginia had given me the chance to live, would not my gratitude have gone to them? Today, when I read about how our country was liberated, the haphazardness of my journeys is even sadder. I explain it to myself by saying that my gratitude mattered to Stalin, but didn't matter so much to Eisenhower, not enough for him to take the risk in that overture to today's confrontation.[3]

In 1949 Šimečka began to study philosophy, Russian, and Czech literature at the university in Brno. After graduating he taught Czech for a year at a combined elementary and secondary school in Kroměříž and

3. Published in the samizdat journal *Obsah*, October 1985, and in Lenka Procházková, ... *a co si o tom myslíte Vy?* (Munich: Obrys/Kontur, 1986), pp. 63-67.

moved to Bratislava in 1954. His career as a university teacher began at the Department of Marxism-Leninism, where his job was to explain the basics of Marxist philosophy to students of medicine and pharmacy. It was there I came to know him a year later, in the autumn of 1955, when by coincidence I found myself at the same department. Of those first months what I remember most is a conversation in his rooms in the student residence hall in Horský Park, probably before Christmas 1955. He confided to me that he could hardly wait for the political earthquake at the upcoming congress in Moscow that had been called for February 1956; he talked about how the Stalin legend was going to get a good licking, which it did.

Nineteen-fifty-six was a stormy year. I recall how each morning Milan would impatiently open the several newspapers that were delivered to the department, and how he would follow news from abroad and openly express himself on the sensational events of those times. And I can still hear the sentence passed on him by one of those nine young men under thirty years of age at the Department of Marxism-Leninism when in Czechoslovakia the year 1956 ended the way it did: "I would get into the trenches with anybody else in this place, Milan, but with you I'd be afraid you'd shoot me in the back!" The person who made this statement was said to be in the secret police's power on account of his alcoholism. And things did not look good in the spring of 1957 either — the greatest dogmatist at the department let it be known that Milan "deserves a year digging ditches." Šimečka was spared this dubious manner of toughening one up by manual labor for thirteen years.

After summer vacation in 1957, he began to teach at the School of the Performing Arts. The next ten years were probably the period of his most intensive study of philosophy, when he became thoroughly acquainted with the substance of the various philosophical schools and systems of the past.[4] It was not only a matter of lectures for students; in late 1959 and early

4. A thorough knowledge of the philosophical literature often proved useful for Šimečka in the 1970s and 1980s, above all when writing *Letters about the Nature of Reality*, composed in Ruzyně prison in the first six months of 1982, which required him to rely entirely on what he could recall of his former studies.

1960 he discovered one of the topics to which he would remain faithful till the end of his life, namely, social utopia.

In his first book, *Sociálne utópie a utopisti* [1961; Social Utopias and Utopians], Šimečka thoroughly charted his terrain. After this preparatory work he went a bit further: in late 1964 he finished the first draft of his *Kríza utopizmu*[5] [The Crisis of Utopianism]. The basis of the ideas here, though now and then camouflaged and terminologically bearing the marks of the period it was written in, is an analysis of how former social utopias resulted in contemporary Marxism. The book, which was finally published in 1967, was a daring act under the then prevailing circumstances in Czechoslovakia. It naturally brought the author a number of difficulties, even at the manuscript stage; one of the guardians of purity of Slovak Marxist philosophy did not want to accept it as Šimečka's postdoctoral thesis. Fortunately it was published at a time when the social crisis of the second half of the 1960s was coming to a head, so the matter blew over without scandal.

At the age of thirty-seven Šimečka had an opportunity to complete his own private university. From the autumn of 1967 to February 1968 he spent six months on a scholarship in the Institute of European History, Mainz. Most of all he was excited by the contemporary Western world and its ideology (the events that were to take place throughout the West in 1968, including the youth revolts in France, Germany, and the United States were just around the corner) and the daily conversations with young people from that half of Europe (including historians, philosophers, and theologians, who were on scholarships at the Institute in Mainz). Later, of course, he was taken with the confrontation between the reality of the Western world and the reality of socialism at home — its propaganda about itself and the West, with which he was intimately acquainted.

After the occupation of Czechoslovakia by the Warsaw Pact forces on August 21, 1968, he wrote a text which was not intended for publication.

See *Dopisy o povaze skutečnosti* published in samizdat with a Foreword by Milan Šimečka, (Prague: Edice Petlice, 1982), 100 pp. typescript.

5. *Kríza utopizmu: O kontinuite a vyústení utopických názorov*, (Bratislava: Obzor, 1967).

One of our Prague friends reckoned that Alexander Dubček might be interested in the opinions of intellectuals and that it would be useful to write an independent and open view of the situation prevailing in the country. Milan quickly wrote a private commentary on the situation in Czechoslovakia and a prognosis of the direction events might take; years later the commentary lacks none of its original brilliance:

> The authority of today's leaders is tremendous but it is also easily shakeable . . . It is based purely on sympathy for moral rectitude, not on sympathy for a program. All that is needed for this popularity to come crashing down is a bit of hypocrisy, the sacrificing of some people or anything else. Therein lies the perfidy of the Moscow agreements. In essence they are a matter of Moscow's policy being executed by people who became popular precisely by having set themselves against it. [...] The position of our leaders is schizophrenic. The people today are watching and waiting, and the time will come when they will shrug it off. [...] A creeping restoration might appear. That would mean the ultimate betrayal. Authority would gradually diminish, almost unobserved, and dissipate into passivity. The people would then search elsewhere for another way out. The last hope of socialism in Czechoslovakia, socialism as an order not as state ownership of the means of production, would then die. The Communist Party would thereby have written itself out of the history of Czechoslovakia. The Moscow agreements constitute instructions for this creeping restoration; they need only remain in force three years. This development would then leave a catastrophic taint on the self-confidence of the nation and the national character.[6]

In May 1969 it was clear that his worst fears were being confirmed, that the creeping restoration of totalitarianism was underway and quickly gaining speed. In a letter sent to a friend abroad Šimečka discussed this freely, though one senses desperation in his words: "I'm in high dudgeon

6. Vilém Prečan, *Die sieben Jahre von Prag 1969–1976. Briefe und Dokumente aus der Zeit der „Normalisierung,"* (Frankfurt: Fischer, 1978). It was first published in full in Milan Šimečka, "Od ledna do srpna: Soukromý komentář k situaci, odevzdaný v září 1969 sekretariátu Alexandra Dubčeka," *Listy*, 21.6 (1991), pp. 12-14.

because today Husák was on television jumping about at a Party meeting in Vysočany. He is quite clearly a psychopath. He managed to make statements that were strongly reminiscent of the croaks of a troglodyte from the 1950s. [...] The scum and the dirt rise slowly to the top, impotent men and idiots with complexes shake about on the screen and babble their bullshit. I'm amazed I was once in the same party with those people. What we predicted has actually happened. The Party has once and for all discredited itself, and has become simply a fifth column."

It was another nine months before the mechanism of normalization took the form of existential violence. On the day of his fortieth birthday, March 6, 1970, after having been thrown out of the Party, Šimečka was dismissed from the university. From the autumn of 1970 till his arrest in May 1981, he worked at various jobs: a year as a chauffeur, a number of years as a power shovel operator, and after a dramatic event when, owing to poorly drawn plans, his power shovel dug up a high tension cable, he decided to give up that job to become a production manager in a cement factory.

For at least five years, beginning in the autumn of 1969, he wrote nothing that was intended for publication in any form. He did, however, write a number of letters, some of which have survived. Before emigrating in 1976 I had microfilms made of our correspondence, and they were smuggled abroad. A number of the letters could therefore be published in German translation in *Die Sieben Jahre von Prag*. These letters are authentic, first-rate contemporaneous testimony about how those who had shaken off their juvenile belief in Communist utopia and were now shedding the last remnants of Marxist and pseudo-Marxist ideology were continuing to mature, both politically and as people in general, detailing their "woe from wit" and their search for a meaningful existence.

At that time, of course, Šimečka was feeling particularly frustrated, not so much on account of the meaningless work he was engaged in as because of passive resistance. "Sometimes I get so furious," he wrote on January 4, 1972, "that I could punch a completely innocent person in the mouth, simply because he is unable to understand how difficult it is to lead this rotten existence." He began to complain that he was becoming repulsed by the written word he himself would put on paper. Similarly, on July 12, 1972 he wrote: "I stare at the typewriter as if it were a strange object . . . and am amazed when recalling that I once used to write every day."

At the time he was determined to change jobs, intending to take a course for power shovel operators. "Thank God that I'm such a bear of a man," he wrote, "and that I now have exactly the kind of belly that truck drivers have. I don't have to make my appearance conform. And I have no difficulty using foul language with the correct accent, the one that distinguishes the naturally boorish man of the people from the intellectual boor. Things will be fine." But they weren't. A year later, in mid-June, he wrote the following about his state of mind:

> The supply of patience is slowly being exhausted. Mine too is nearly run out, when, for instance, I notice the difficulty the process of writing causes me. My hands are paralyzed as if by a stroke. And it's all because of those wretched machines. And I say to myself that they ought to do something before they become completely paralyzed. I also know what is destroying us. It's the passivity which we have in part voluntarily entered and in part been cast in to; but what is worse for this subjective state is that we have, after careful consideration, voluntarily accepted it as the attitude that best corresponds to the period.

• • •

The last fifteen years of Milan Šimečka's life is the period that is perhaps best known. It was increasingly filled with writing, and we now have an extensive bibliography of his work from these years,[7] which provides us with an opportunity to recall the range and sheer volume of his output as well as the number of languages his books and essays were translated into.

---

7. See Milan Drápala with Vilém Prečan, *Milan Šimečka: Předběžná bibliografie díla za léta 1975–1990*, Prague and Scheinfeld-Schwarzenberg: Institute of Contemporary History and the Czechoslovak Documentation Centre, 1991.

The entire period, from 1975 till the revolution of 1989, can be divided into several phases. These phases are markedly different from one another owing to the circumstances in which his work emerged (whether it related solely to his own life or to the broader social events), and also to their thematic orientation. Šimečka's thirteen-month detention on remand, from May 6, 1981 to May 27, 1982, constitutes the most important watershed in his life.

In the first six-year period, before his imprisonment, he wrote approximately ten articles, two books — *Obnovení pořádku: Příspěvek k typologii reálného socialismu* [*The Restoration of Order*][8] and, with Miroslav Kusý, *Veľký brat a veľka sestra* [Big Brother and Big Sister] — the long essay "Společenství strachu" [Community of Fear], the essay "československé Polsko, polské Československo" [Czechoslovak Poland and Polish Czechoslovakia], and the Forward to the Italian edition of *The Restoration of Order.* In addition, he began the article "Náš soudruh Winston Smith" [Our comrade W.S.]. In these works he came to terms with the past and went to the threshold of the present. Up till the time of his imprisonment, while working as a manual laborer, he was able to write only after work, on the weekend, and during vacation. This changed considerably after his return from prison.

I talked to him by telephone twenty minutes after he had arrived in Bratislava from Prague, immediately following his release, and then very frequently and in great detail in the days to come. I was interested to know how his experience of prison manifested itself in his attitudes as compared to before.

He didn't talk about prison — not then, nor later. Rather, he talked about the same thing his letters from prison were abundant in: the value of love and friendship. He advocated tolerance and understanding, he railed against pettiness, forbade his friends to have conflicts, and could not stand the slightest indication of malice. Perhaps what was most striking was how freely he expressed himself, without concealment,

8. *The Restoration of Order: The Normalization of Czechoslovakia 1969-1976,* translated from the Czech by A. G. Brain (London: Verso, 1984).

without innuendo, without regard for the "ear" of the authorities, which we knew was listening in on our telephone conversations.

From the beginning I ascribed this new degree of openness to the euphoria stemming from his recently achieved freedom. Gradually, however, I came to realize that I was witness to a phenomenon I had seen in others who had returned from "over there." Years before, Šimečka had decided that it was impossible to remain silent and that he would not be a "naked human being who had nothing except himself and his anxiety about the rest of his life and the lives of those close to him." Now, after his return, it was as if he were clinging to his identity as a man more than before his imprisonment: he no longer, for instance, wanted to play the ridiculous game of hide-and-seek with the régime. He rejected any role in a "normalized" world of sham: when his "sickness benefits" ended after his eye operation, he went to look for work at the employment office, expressing the reservation, however, that he would not accept any work that did not correspond to his qualifications. Under suspicion of parasitism, Šímečka was interrogated: he showed the police the statements from the State Bank and insisted that the police report include the information that he was living from modest payments received for publications abroad.

Soon after his return from prison, Šimečka wrote his second addendum to his study of socialist utopias, *Svět s utopiemi, nebo bez nich?* [A world with utopias or without them?]. In 1983 he completed "Our comrade, Winston Smith" and apart from a number of reviews and columns he wrote two serious works, each in a different style, on the arms race and the peace movement — *Balance* and *Válka je vůl* [Down with war]. He also began to write a series of more than fifty column-like pieces which were eventually published together as *Kruhová obrana* [Circular defense].

The post-prison period of Šimečka's work is marked by a quantitative growth in output, not only because he had become a professional writer, but also because of external circumstances, that is, a growing public demand. On the one hand there occurred a boom in samizdat publishing: from as early as 1981 the number of samizdat periodicals grew considerably, and one can safely even call it a publishing explosion after 1984. On the other hand, there were requests from abroad, where Šimečka was soon among the most sought-after independent authors from Czechoslovakia. He was published there not only in émigré journals, but also in numerous newspapers and other periodicals; editors of essay collections as well as conference organizers at universities and elsewhere turned to him for contributions concerning serious contemporary issues. The result is evident from a mere glance at his bibliography: one can, without exaggeration, say that apart from Václav Havel, Milan Šimečka was the most translated Czechoslovak author of nonfiction.

It is clearly beyond the scope of this brief survey to discuss all the subjects of Šimečka's work during the six years leading up to the revolution of 1989. I should, however, like to point to at least three areas with which he was particularly concerned. One was shifts within the sphere of the powers that be, where he concentrated mostly on developments in the Soviet Union. He began a number of articles of this kind, including a commentary written in March 1985 on the ascent of Mikhail Gorbachev to the top post in the Soviet nomenklatura. A work on Czechoslovak current affairs, which, for my own purposes, I describe as "concerning Czechoslovakia's road to freedom," and which Šimečka himself compiled for the volume *Konec nehybnosti* [The end of inertia]. The third thematic group comprised Czech and Slovak independent literature of the 1970s and 1980s. He wrote a number of pieces of criticism, reviews, and annotations, and a radio series that was broadcast by Radio Free Europe. In his acceptance speech at the awarding of the 1986 Palach Prize, he was the one who noted the "miracle of the birth of free culture, which began with ordinary copying paper, old typewriters and . . . the belief that it made sense, that there was a point in doing it, and that it was an effective weapon against lies, oppression, and stupidity." There is a passage from this that deserves to be quoted in full:

> The world that sits down at the television to watch the evening news with its color pictures of wars, demonstrations, famine, and terrorist attacks

is today no longer especially interested in my quiet, disappointed, and apparently apathetic country. And yet it is precisely in this country that I have obtained supreme evidence of the indispensability of the cultural experience that one has actually lived, that gets into your bones. What I eighteen years ago sceptically considered impossible has happened; namely, despite extensive, well-thought-out, and stupid persecution, free arts and culture have developed in our country, with a breadth and a variety we would never have dreamt of. In the years of political immobility, amidst social paralysis, in the community of fear, hundreds of works have been written, which have found their way — written out in the most varied and often poor manner — into the hands of thousands and even, in some cases, tens of thousands of readers. Independent historiography, philosophy, sociology, and the rest of the scholarly disciplines that need no laboratory or workshop have held their own and even developed. The music of the young could not be held back, plays for the stage have been written and performed in private apartments, dozens of journals have been publishing in such a variety of orientations and range of opinions that one is astounded. Our friends in exile have cultivated another branch of this free culture and have also established institutions, journals, publishing houses, archives, and foundations. And all of that was born spontaneously, without thinking about hard times, without material impetuses and without office staffs — simply of a social need, of the fabulous ideas and industriousness of thousands of people . . . All of this was born after the shock of hopelessness and desperation: the arts and culture protected themselves with a narrower solidarity, but one that was therefore all the more solid.[9]

Over this fifteen-year period, from 1975 to 1990, Milan Šimečka created an extensive body of work, which in sum is an important component of contemporary Czech and Slovak thinking, as well as part of the message that we are sending out from our corner of Europe to the rest of the world.

9. Quoted from a manuscript, an excerpt of which appeared in *Listy*, 17.2 (April 1987).

• • •

What is the best way to characterize Milan Šimečka's work? What are the ideas contained in it? This cannot be answered in a single sentence or with an enumeration of the topics he was concerned with. Moreover, it is intimately connected with his life, and in a certain sense, in fact, it stems from his life. His work is polythematic, and though it has several levels it also has a common denominator, and no one level can be separated from the other two.

In other words, it is a body of work about our era and its great history, about man — that is to say, about the nature of his reality and about his little history, as well as about the continuous oscillation of man between great and small history, about how these histories intertwine, how these poles of the same reality are interconnected. It is ultimately a work about Šimečka's reality and the reality of Šimečka.

He was an interpreter of our era. His work is dominated by our ever living and omnipresent past of the last fifty years, if not longer, including the historical basis on which this past was played out, and by everything that forms the fleeting present and, to a certain extent, also codetermines our uncertain future. In other words, it is a work about the history of this era. Not a single one of the great milestones or questions of this history is missing. All the dilemmas of the era have here been charted out and named, all the junctures, all the places where the points on the tracks have irrevocably been thrown; we find here all the figures who co-created this era of our present. And without exception we would probably find all the themes of our unmastered past, providing they extend into the present: Munich, Beneš, Germans, Jews, Slovakia, the post-war pro-Soviet infatuation, and the circumstances related to the establishment of the Communist totalitarian régime and its maintenance for more than forty years.

In no way is it the usual scholarly historiography. It is not political history, and even less so is it narrative history (except perhaps for the historical excursion *Ztráty skutečnosti* [Losses of reality]). Šimečka's work was close to the so-called "history of problems" in that it took an interdisciplinary approach to methodology. Research results were incorporated from all the disciplines concerned with man and reality in the broadest sense (psychology, philosophy, economics, sociology, political science). Nor did he work as a professional historian with footnotes (which in and of themselves constitute merely an external attribute of an historical work, often designed to dupe the less–informed). Šimečka's perception of reality and his thinking were historical; his approach to the analysis of social phenomena and the destinies of nations and individual people was historical. He started from the given context of a period and the roots of each reality and each human act in that context, which were conditioned by the existing state of knowledge, awareness, mentality, and interests.

He liked to use his own terminology, which he derived from his own conception of human reality, namely the term "great history." Great history is in his view the determination of man by the social and political system, the determination by forces that attempt to turn man into their object, to manipulate him, to force their will upon him, to control him, to make him submissive. One could, I believe, also talk about "great politics" without making too much of a jump from what Šimečka had in mind with his "great history," especially when one takes great politics to mean as well the politics of the totalitarian state, the analysis of which was at the heart of much of his shorter and lengthier works.

Šimečka, however, also exposed what was often hidden behind great history, and he did so in two respects. He criticized the hypertrophied state and its power, that is, the power structures pretending that their interests were those of the whole society, the people, the nation. He repeatedly chose as the target of his criticism the militant ideology and ideological constructions sanctifying great history that "continuously tries to roll us along its riverbed as if we were pebbles." And again and again he pointed to the role played in great history and great politics by quite ordinary motifs from the small, personal history of man: ambition, fear of the future, envy, hope, obedience.

Politics in Šimečka's work is submitted to careful scrutiny not only as great history — the state, power, the external determination of man — but also in the original analytical sense, that is, as a matter of public affairs, as an attempt at citizenship with full rights, in the meaning that regained import in our totalitarian-filled era — politics as the attempt to be one's self, to have the freedom to say that two times two equals four.

It would not, however, be quite right to limit the scope of Šimečka the philosopher only to politics. I have come to the conclusion that one should not be reluctant to talk about him as a philosopher without any other qualifiers. The matter of his philosophy is similar to that of his history. Šimečka did not intend to make his mark in the world of academic philosophy; in any event, he didn't have the professional resources at his disposal for that. And yet he was a philosopher in the original sense of the word — he investigated the world as a whole, and the questions which were at the center of his interest and flashed at the background of his investigation of the phenomena he wrote about have ranked among the basic questions of philosophy since its beginning. The difficulty, however, is the form in which he would present his inquiry and his answers: "when philosophy was not yet ashamed of simplicity and comprehensibility and even of a certain naivety when asking questions."

In his work Šimečka's own state of being was tossed about between public history (which, as he once wrote, had dealt him a blow or two), and his private history, the main content of which was the chain reaction of self-liberation and the carrying out of the duties of the intellectual as he himself understood them: "at the very least to describe the situation in the social community in which one lives." The history of his writing, of the basic content and purpose of his life, is also the story of how his private history, developing within the small community of independent intellectuals, helped to prepare the change in public history, the restoration of freedom in our country.

That is far from a full explanation of what Šimečka gave us with his work and what he left behind as the lasting key to understanding the period. He was an interpreter of our era not only because he provided information or a sum of knowledge; above all he helped one to understand everyday life. Nor would it be correct to call him a chronicler of our times. Rather, he taught us to understand the world in which we lived, he explained the logic behind what seemed to be illogical, nonsensical, against all nature and common sense, and he answered the question "Why?". He did all of this by means that remain intelligible even to the reader who has never heard of philosophy, never read a single scholarly book on history, and is not particularly knowledgeable about this field.

Šimečka made no attempt to hide the fact that he was presenting his own vision of reality, that he was sharing with us his own personal knowledge. He rejected the existence of what is sometimes called "objective reality." Analyzing the destructiveness and catastrophic consequences of any kind of ideological blindness, he started from the position that "all ideological motives of historical action were sanctified with objectivity; without that sanctification those motives would have been impossible."

He presented his vision of reality and his own reality with great refinement, as a literary artist. The result was a miracle of communication between author and reader. Not only was he able to name what we had so far only vaguely sensed, and in a way that we suddenly understood, he also wrote in a way that made reading his work pleasurable.

But even that is not the whole secret of how his writing spoke to us, enraptured us, and left its mark on us. In one of his letters he wrote something to the effect: "I approve of every interpretation of the world that can help us towards kindness; every interpretation of the world that does not reproduce fear is good."

Šimečka's writing spoke not only to our reason, but also to our hearts, more precisely, to our better "selves." Even when writing about the less than savory sides of our lives, about the ugliness and monstrosity of the Communist system, his words were free of hatred. On the contrary, his writing never lacked an appeal to the human desire for good, understanding, love, and friendship, a desire so indestructibly present in every human being.

—Vilém Prečan

TRANSLATOR'S NOTE

I have felt a deep affinity with Milan Šimečka ever since I read his seminal study of totalitarian rule *The Restoration of Order* on my return to England from Prague in 1980. It was to be the first of his writings I would translate over the following decade. The English translation of this book was to play a unique role in explaining to many in the West how it was possible that the people who had protested courageously and in unity against the Soviet invasion of 1968 appeared to accept docilely a primitive neo-Stalinism after enjoying a period of relative freedom.

That translation and the subsequent ones were published under my pseudonym A.G. Brain, which I had invented in the fond hope that Big Brother (or BB as Milan used to write) would not connect me with this "subversive" literature. (At the time I was making regular trips between London and Prague as a courier, bearing messages from the Czech exiles to the democratic opposition.)

I did not meet Milan in person until 1985, when I was able to discover for myself that the man and his writings were one, and experience the enormous warmth of his personality. As I translated more and more of his commentaries on the contemporary state of Czech, Slovak, and European society I came to regard him as a columnist in the best tradition of I.F. Stone, Art Buchwald and George Orwell, whose writings he was to champion in his own country. However, unlike those authors he was fated to be a journalist without a newspaper. His "columns" would appear regularly in the samizdat monthly review *Obsah*. It is to be regretted that none of his collected essays have yet to be published in English, particularly the collection *Circular Defense* written in 1984, a year full of symbolic meaning for him especially.

Many among the dissidents found his analyses naively optimistic. As an avid reader of Russian he closely monitored the changes in Russia following the rise to power of Mikhail Gorbachev and thus had rare insights into changes within the bloc. He shared with Václav Havel the ability to conceive of the imminent restoration of freedom (as he entitled his first essay in 1990) amidst general scepticism, although there were even moments, such as in 1987, when he too voiced despondency at the failure of *glasnost* to have any knock-on effect in the Soviet sattelites.

Šimečka's thirteen-month detention in 1981-82 was part of a crackdown by the regime in the face of the first cracks in the edifice of normalization. It was a time when no one in Czechoslovakia could have been blamed for seeing no hope of change on the horizon and people concerned themselves almost exclusively with their own private lives. This was not the case of Milan Šimečka, as is evident throughout his letters from prison.

Milan Šimečka died an untimely death in 1990. As a Czech living in Slovakia who "went native" to the extent that he also wrote widely in Slovak, he was devastated by the separatist fervor that started to be felt in Slovakia immediately after the fall of the Communist regime and eventually led to the break-up of the Czech and Slovak Federative Republic. In a very true sense he can be said to have died of a broken heart. He was therefore never to write his memoirs, and his prison letters constitute almost the only autobiographical material available about this remarkable man. In many ways that was the idea that guided me as I made my selection from the thirty or more lengthy letters that have survived.

However, they are clearly not simply an autobiographical work but are also a moving testimony to human courage in adversity (we must bear in mind that he had no idea when he would be released and his detention was repeatedly renewed), and as such form part of that distinguished tradition of prison writing. Though no believer in the conventional sense, he demonstrates on almost every page an undying hope that would be the envy of many a Christian. (Writing at the same period about the former communists who were imprisoned with him in the fifties, the Catholic priest and Charter 77 signatory Josef Zvěřina said "I thank them for the depth of their conscience and their courage which has frequently given me strength. It is painful for me to admit that seldom have I encountered 'such faith in Israel.'")

Clearly the letters do not constitute a "work" in the sense of Václav Havel's *Letters to Olga*. The author never knew if the letters would reach their destination — and indeed a significant number of them did not. On the other hand, they are not a succession of disparate letters but an ongoing dialogue.

Because I adopted a thematic approach in making my selection, the inclusion of salutations seemed to me inappropriate. Among the main themes present throughout the letters is his relationship with the different members of his family: his wife Eva (Muki), his sons Petr and Milan, his sister Ila, and his late brother Fredo. They reflect the intensity of his personal relationships, which was almost overpowering in the case of his marriage.

Not surprisingly, the other main theme in the letters is philosophy, and indeed his philosophical reflections are inseparable from his family correspondence. Addressing his wife, Eva, in one of the letters he recalls how he had overcome his own existential crisis six years earlier by starting to write — freely, albeit without hope of publication. It was a man determined to defend his intellectual freedom who confronted his interrogators with courage in those first months of his imprisonment.

At no moment does he cease to engage philosophically with his surroundings, and in the best phenomenological and existentialist traditions, philosophical discourse and literature are intertwined. Not only was literature a constant source of inspiration, but his own writing is of a very high literary standard. Unforgettable is his description of time: "It's like glue; it sticks to my fingers and my soul. I suddenly perceive it as a living creature with a slimy, indolent body that lounges around here, filling the narrow space until it's impossible to breathe."

However, he did pen a series of letters devoted solely to philosophy — "Letters about the Nature of Reality." Addressed to his sons and written without any resources but his own memory, they are a tour de force of philosophical writing. It is to be hoped that his key writings on utopianism, written before he was silenced, will also be published in English before too long.

—Gerald Turner ("A.G. Brain")
Prague, October 2001

About the Contributors

Vilém Prečan is a historian. After emigrating to Germany in 1976 he established the Documentation Centre for the Promotion of Independent Czechoslovak Literature and was instrumental in publishing dissident writers abroad.

Jiřina Šiklová is a sociologist and teaches at Charles University in Prague. A former key figure in the dissident movement, she is the director of the Gender Studies Program.

Gerald Turner, originally from England, has translated a number of works of modern Czech fiction, including *Judge on Trial* by Ivan Klíma, *Bringing up Girls in Bohemia* by Michal Viewegh, and *Czech Dreambook* by Ludvík Vaculík (yet to be published). In addition, he is the translator of Milan Šimečka's *The Restoration of Order* (London: Verso, 1984). He lives in Prague.

LETTERS FROM PRISON

MILAN ŠIMEČKA

Selected and translated from the Czech and Slovak by Gerald Turner • Originally published as *Listy z väzenia / Dopisy z vězení*, edited by Jolana Kusá and Raisa Kopsová (Bratislava: Milan Šimečka Foundation, 1999) • This edition first published in 2002 by Twisted Spoon Press, P.O. Box 21 — Preslova 12, 150 21 Prague 5, Czech Republic, www.twistedspoon.com • Printed in the Czech Republic by Tiskárny Havlíčkův Brod • Text set in Janson • Cover photo appears courtesy of the Milan Šimečka Foundation • Grateful acknowledgment is made to Samuel Abrahám, Dagmar Kusá, Jolana Kusá, and Lenka Procházková for their assistance, to Jeffrey Young for his careful editing, and to James Ottaway for his generous support • Distributed to the trade in North America by SCB DISTRIBUTORS: 15608 South New Century Drive, Gardena, CA 90248, 1-800-729-6423, www.scbdistributors.com